Memories

Frasinia R. Dolack

TRAFFORD
PUBLISHING™

Note for Librarians: a cataloguing record for this book that includes Dewey Decimal Classification and US Library of Congress numbers is available from the Library and Archives of Canada. The complete cataloguing record can be obtained from their online database at: www.collectionscanada.ca/amicus/index-e.html
ISBN 1-4251-1225-0

TRAFFORD
PUBLISHING

Offices in Canada, USA, Ireland and UK
This book was published *on-demand* in cooperation with Trafford Publishing. On-demand publishing is a unique process and service of making a book available for retail sale to the public taking advantage of on-demand manufacturing and Internet marketing. On-demand publishing includes promotions, retail sales, manufacturing, order fulfilment, accounting and collecting royalties on behalf of the author.

Book sales for North America and international:
Trafford Publishing, 6E–2333 Government St.,
Victoria, BC v8t 4p4 CANADA
phone 250 383 6864 (toll-free 1 888 232 4444)
fax 250 383 6804; email to orders@trafford.com
Book sales in Europe:
Trafford Publishing (uk) Ltd., Enterprise House, Wistaston Road Business Centre,
Wistaston Road, Crewe, Cheshire cw2 7rp UNITED KINGDOM
phone 01270 251 396 (local rate 0845 230 9601)
facsimile 01270 254 983; orders.uk@trafford.com
Order online at:
trafford.com/06-2984

10 9 8 7 6 5 4 3 2 1

Thank you to my daughter Marlene Willey and family friend Ann Lindberg for their assistance.

TO MY FAMILY

CONTENTS

GLORIOUS SUNSET

As I sit on the patio and admire the beautiful Arizona sunset— my thoughts seem to float off into space and take on different heavenly shadows that are so true to life. Some of the colorings are so beautiful that it thrills my very soul, and the dark shadows are like the pitfalls and stresses through life that shake the very foundation of our universe. How many moons, days, hours, and minutes have gone by—my thoughts seem to review before my eyes.

"Which is the most important one to begin with?"

Well, each one seems important to me. Yes, each day seems like the day before, but it's really not so, for we are a day older and gain that much more of life, and we should be wiser if we store each gain as a lesson that we receive each day. We may not, however, see it that way at the time.

Gradually, the evening blends into the night and the silhouette of trees turn into ebony lace—etching against the horizon. With this glorious view before me, it brings me back to my childhood days. They were wonderful days! We were loved very much—that I am sure of—more each day, as life unreels before me.

Our parents lived by the Ten Commandments. We were brought up in such a home. Too bad that many children do not have that fortunate privilege these days. Each one of us had duties to perform no matter how poorly they were done at the time. As we grew older, our jobs improved and more was added to our daily chores. Oh, yes, we had time for play too. Work had to be finished on Saturday by the setting sun. Sundays we were reprieved from work (only the most essential—like milking cows and feeding the living creatures and tending to their comforts) in order to respect the Sabbath day.

Our duties increased as we grew older, but before that we had many happy hours to play and get into mischief, as all healthy and creative boys and girls do. But mind you, our mischief and creativity were analyzed for our own good before it got out of hand. What surprised us most was how mama and daddy knew. We were so discreet—at least, that was what we thought.

Another day has gone by and I am adding more of my memories of days gone by to the pages of the book I plan to write. Wish me luck!

I recall very vividly our goodbyes to relatives and friends before departing to America. The year was 1913. Why it registers so strongly in my mind, I don't know, as I recall nothing else until I was almost four years old. Everyday stresses of a child were easily forgotten—especially if the pains were kissed away or soothed by people who loved you.

The next experience that I remember, even today, was when mother gave me to hold my baby sister Raya, while she was attending to her many duties. Raya couldn't have been more than nine months old, as mother was still nursing her. I put my arms around Raya. We were both seated on the door of a root cellar. It had rained hard the night before and left many small pools of water. I was watching the pigs and other farm animals enjoying themselves in it.

A big mother pig came along and grabbed Raya away from me and started to run for one of the puddles. I screamed, "Mama, help!" Mama was sweeping at the time. She ran out with the broom and aimed it like a spear. What marksmanship! She hit the pig square on its hind quarters. The pig opened its mouth to grunt with pain and surprise. Baby Raya fell to the ground within inches of the puddle. Mother ran over and picked Raya up, nursed her quiet and then handed Raya back to me to hold. (Now—I can understand mama's calm and quick reaction to the situation.)

Mother had always taken life in stride and met everything with chin up—even death—as I recall. Well, at least Raya was not the

worst for her experience and the day went, but not without its usual
few dramatic moments.

SAD DAY FOR THE WEASEL

My brother Bill discovered a weasel in the chicken coop. I can assure you—it was not the weasel's day. It ran into the woodpile for safety, but not for long, as Letz's army stationed themselves around the woodpile with patience, if need be, for days. The poor weasel darted out to run, only to be taken as the big trophy of the day and to be viewed by our father Gregory Letz. He looked at the weasel and then at his army. Father's smile was our reward—then he muttered under his breath, "The poor creature did not have a chance."

Oh, did I tell you that we were a family of 15 children—and four others adopted? Just a bit more than a baker's dozen and each one had their own spicy flavor. No dull moments in our household. Yes, there was illness, bruises and hurt prides—which seemed to disappear as days and years passed.

Dad and mother put their big family out on a mixed farm. It held everything imaginable—fowl of all species, cattle, horses, sheep, goats, cats and dogs. Different kinds of grains were raised to feed men and beasts. A wonderful garden—was a necessary addition. Each bug was given personal attention and informed why they were not wanted—generally a rock treatment was used.

Water seemed to have played a very important part in our world. It held a very important roll in our lives too. Father made a reservoir— just digging a hole in the ground was not enough— a dam had to be built. Father lined up his army to help clear the land of rocks. We all bent over and threw the rocks between our legs. Slowly, our efforts began to show. Long piles of rocks lined the field and they were hauled away later to be put into the makings of a dam.

Many happy times were spent when winter came and froze the

water over. We could skate or play games on it; it answered many needs. Since cattle drank from it, a well had to be dug and water hauled in from Teton River (eight miles from home) for drinking water. Barrels were used to haul the water in the good old days!

When dad came here the first time, he filed for the land that the Government was giving out in 160 acre parcels. If one proved on the land for five years it was theirs. This is where dad brought us to. The land was located one mile east of Brady, Montana, which was a small town mostly supplying the farmers' needs. If one wished to buy of more luxury, he'd have to travel over one hundred miles. This took quite some time with horse and buggy. The land soon turned into a mixed farm. The folks raised everything imaginable for the many needs of daily living so far from nowhere in time of slow traveling.

Mother felt like the farm was at the end of the world. The only thing that kept her going was that God was near. She said that she didn't know that any human being was in sight until—from their curiosity—hardly a day went by that someone did not drop in to see the Russian family that settled there. It seemed that our arrival traveled far and wide. They were amazed, since they envisioned that Russians were dark people, and we were very white.

BAKING BREAD

Mr. Peterson, our neighbor south of us, came to talk with dad about something. It was mother's bread baking day—(first time in the American coal range). She proceeded to use the same method as she would in homemade brick ovens. She heated the oven until it was real hot, put the bread in and let the fire die down.

"Mrs. Letz, are you baking, by any chance?" Mr. Peterson asked.

"Yes, bread," she said.

"You have to keep the fire going in this kind of stove in order to bake," he said.

Mother thanked him kindly. Of course this communication required an interpreter which my brother Jim did quite well, as he'd come to America on dad's first trip here with the older family. Besides mother had a dream that there would be a horrible war a year before they decided to come to America. I am sure happy they came here.

It wasn't long after that, that dad built mother a big baking oven in one end of the kitchen and they used the other stove too—just like the one she had in Russia. It had many uses. The top of it was for sleeping or drying out wet children's clothes. It was like a big fireplace except deep like the width of a double bed and as long. It was used for all sorts of cooking, as only mother knew from —way back. We were taught how to use it too. Many times mother would help me into it when it was cold to sweep out the ashes and put them into a bucket which was then carried out on the garden patch and mixed with the soil. Straw and wood were used to start the fire and then coal added to make a bed of hot coals to start baking or cooking. If the coal ran short—the folks had other means to cook and keep warm. Dry cattle droppings were picked up and stored in a shed to keep dry and to be used when needed. That was a job for all summer.

May 30, 1914 mother gave birth to a baby boy—with only dad's help. They named him Maurice. He was a beautiful baby. I recall people stopping in. (It was not unusual those days as distances were far and people would stop for a drink of water for themselves or their horses, or maybe an overnight rest.) And they would rave about his beauty. He had green eyes, golden curly hair and most perfect baby features, and he grew up to be a very handsome man.

In the year of 1916 on August 29th, we had our last addition to the family. Mother was 49 years old. Another little boy and truly, he, too, was beautiful, with big blue eyes and straight blonde hair. Daddy helped mother again. Of course he called the elder girls to come in and clean up the baby and mother.

GEORGE

George started his artistic career at the very tender age of three. Mother would give him a pair of dull painted scissors and paper to keep him amused while she did her work. He would have the window panes covered with cutouts of birds, rabbits, chickens, etc.—free hand. If there wasn't any dew on the pane, he'd use his saliva to make them stick, but that was seldom necessary in winter time, as Jack Frost provided framing for his cutouts which would last for days, or until the sun decided to warm things up—then they would slide down onto the window ledge.

When we would come home from school, George would be so happy to show us what he had done while we were away. We were proud of our little brother and praised him; he deserved the praise. We even took some of his cutouts to show off at school.

Mother said he would be so wrapped up in his work that hours would pass by and he was not even aware that he was being checked on. She would have to stop him to have lunch.

This genius grew up to be a man I am proud of to this day—actor, painter, motion picture producer, script writer, architect, cabinet maker, sculptor and so many other hobbies. One could write a book just about him. He is such a famous man.

He built his home on Sierra Mar Drive, Los Angeles, California. It overlooked the great Metropolis that looked like a great gem below when the lights were turned on at night. The home was like an eagle's nest that had a view far and wide.

GEORGE ON A FARM

George lived on one big mixed up farm with his mama, daddy, and brothers and sisters. There was always something going on and plenty to do on the farm. His mama just loved to raise everything, as she, too, was a nature lover like George. She raised turkeys, chickens, guinea fowl, geese, ducks, pigeons, bantam chickens, pigs, dogs, cats, cows, horses and sheep. They were friendly with each other and shared their food when they were fed.

George carried grains of wheat in his pockets so he could feed them often. They became good friends and he would pat them. The pigeons would fly down and sit on his head, or shoulders. This made him so happy he'd laugh with delight. Oh yes, he even got to carry them in his hands and listen to them coo. When he would sit on the ground the grain would run out of his pockets. To get the grain, they would walk up on his legs and lap. Oh, that really made him happy; they would look up at him and he could look into their eyes. They were not a bit afraid of him.

There was so much fun in the summer time. When winter came George would have to bundle up in warm clothes to go outside. His mama or daddy would take him outside to see all the animals and fowl. Of course when school was out, then he had his brothers and sisters to play with. He was such a busy little boy that he never seemed lonely.

There were days when a blizzard would last for days, but George kept busy making cutouts for the windows. So when a chinook came and the cutouts slid down the window sill, George would pick them up and try to dry them; he just never had time to be lonely, as you can see.

I think every little girl and boy who gets a chance to live on a farm is fortunate. Wouldn't you like to live on a farm?

THREE RAG DOLLS

Their names were Ephrasinia, Raissa and Heesha. They were happy rag dolls. How would I know—when they could not talk? They had a smile on their lips and twinkle in their eyes. Who would not be happy; their little playmates loved them very much. Oh, yes, they were put to rest at times, but most of the time they were cuddled and carried around on the big mixed up farm to see all the animals and the chickens. They were told what each thing was. It was nice to know all those things even if you couldn't talk.

At the end of the day the rag dolls went to bed with their playmates and received a good night kiss on their little rag faces. Oh, how nice to be loved.

One night when their playmates were asleep something happened. The rag dolls sat up and looked around. Why this never happened before. They smiled at each other and moved their hands and feet. My, this was fun—getting up slowly so as not to awaken their playmates. It only lasted for a few minutes before it was daylight. I am sure it was a dream. "What do you think?"

STICK PEOPLE

I hurried with my chores one morning, as it was such a beautiful day and I wanted to go for a walk in the woods.

"My, you are doing your work up fast this morning," dad said.

"Are you going somewhere?"

"Yes, I'd like to spend a day in the woods."

"I'd sure like to go with you, but mother has plans to go shopping, so we'll be driving into town today," dad said.

"Is there anything you would like us to get you?"

"Thanks dad, but I can't think of anything right now."

"Enjoy yourself, but be careful daughter, as there are many unpleasant things too."

Mother had lunch fixed for me, so I said goodbye to dad and mother and left with my faithful dog, Shep.

The warm dazzling sun was up-high by now, so we decided to rest awhile under the big oak tree overlooking the most beautiful, fragrant valley filled with tall green grass and wildflowers of all colors! Shep must have decided to take a nap—well, I just closed my eyes, but not for long, as I heard a soft crackling noise. I sat up quickly. As for Shep, his eyes were bulging and his ears stood up! We both just could not believe what was happening before our eyes!!

There was a marching parade of what seemed to be wooden sticks. Now, you may find this hard to believe, but they stopped and looked at us and then turned and marched on. For a second, I thought, maybe we dreamed it all. Laughing softly to myself, boy! What a silly dream.

Shep was still a bit perplexed. I could tell by the look in his eyes, so I decided this was as good a time as any to have lunch and what better place could we find.

"What about some lunch, Shep?"

He wagged his tail for an answer; then he walked up to me to share my lunch. I threw the crumbs to the birds, and the birds joyfully enjoyed them.

Low and behold the marching sticks were coming back—right past us again! This was no dream—but hard to believe! The one on the tail end must have been an adventuresome one—he came up to us, smiled and winked; then he turned and ran to catch up with the line of marchers. Shep must have been in shock as he did not make a move or any noise. As for me, well, I thought, I just can not tell this to my folks! Gosh, first thing I know they would take me to a doctor.

Shep and I made quite a few trips into the woods that summer and saw the "Stick People" marching, or just walking around. They were friendly with us and were not afraid. We followed them one day and found out where they lived. They lived in a big pine tree with wide drooping branches down to the ground.

You can be sure, we were careful as to where we stepped for fear of stepping on one of them. There was always someone as a sentry on lookout for birds, as they would snatch the babies and fly away with them. Goodness, everybody seems to have someone to fear as an enemy.

Shep and I had many pleasant outings in the woods and surprises through the summer, but not like the "Stick People". That was one secret we kept to ourselves even to this day.

SCHOOL BEGINS

Little did we know that our carefree days were soon to end—School! Mother and dad had been informed by the school district that all school age children must go to school.

There were seven of us attending the first day of school. We caused quite a controversy amongst the children. They found us rather unusual compared to themselves—really, only in style of clothes and oh, yes, language which we found out later. Of course they were different to us too, but we were so dumbfounded that we could only stare at them with a loss of communication. This predicament we had never been in before. But, I must say, we were more polite. Bless our American teacher (Mrs. Marsh); she helped us breech the gap and brought about a happy medium.

Our names seemed to amuse the children very much. There was one particular boy (Willard Peterson) that singled me out to tease. Hardly a day would go by without tears on my part.

"What is your name?" he would ask me.

"Frasinia, "I said.

I tried helping him pronounce it correctly. After doing this a few times and realizing that this was done to hold other children's attention, I'd give him a cold look and go into the school room and take my seat or practice my A-B-C's on the black board.

"Frasinia, why are you not playing outside with the other children?" Mrs. Marsh asked.

I tried telling her the best I could. She went outside and got the rest of the details. The whole class was called in early. She started by saying,

"I have been noticing that you children have not been very kind to our foreign friends. I had hoped that you children would take pride in learning their names as they have yours. But I see what I must do. I shall give them all new names."

You could have heard a pin drop. Mrs. Marsh proceeded in calling out names. It went so fast and smoothly, as if planned for quite sometime.

"Fraisina will be Rose, Raya—Lyda, Olya—Olga,Wasily—William or Bill, Mischel—Mike, Nicolu—Nick, and Uhiem—Jim.

"I do not want anymore teasing, but learn the new names. Now, we shall resume our class work," she said.

Things took form more humorously, but the mischief—this prevailed in the souls of the children. Willard took up other means to tease me—filling my hat with dirt, or throwing snowballs down the back of my neck. (He was an exhibitor at heart, don't you think?) Until one day I got real brave and strong. I washed his face with snow. He was laughing so he became an easy prey. But this outburst of bravery did bring me a few new friends. The teacher was standing by watching—this sort of game she forbade, but I think she thought he had had it coming for a long time and did not say anything. She even helped me brush the snow off my clothes—with a faint smile about her lips. Willard walked away sheepishly.

The school year went by fast after the children started to accept us. We taught them a few games that they did not know and we learned many of theirs.

Since, our schoolhouse was five miles from our home we had to go by horse and buggy. It was a single horse buggy. It had one seat in the front and room in the back—bottom of the buggy—which seated four of us small children nicely.

Each new day was a challenge to us children. After chores were done and breakfast eaten—we were on our way to school—bundled—of course, according to the weather. This particular morning it was cold! It just so happened that Jim, Nick and Mike could not go to school that morning, as they had to locate some stray horses. Anything that pertained to livelihood had to be taken care of first. Bill was to drive to school that morning which gave him the responsibility he so greatly enjoyed. Sister Olga and Bill took the front seat and Raya and I sat in the back covered up snuggly and cozily. They had the lap robe in the front wrapped around their legs and lap.

Dad was giving Bill last minute instructions, "Son, you know that Star is a gentle horse, but he is afraid of his own shadow. Drive careful and don't try to show off, so you can control him."

As the sun rose higher in the sky, it turned the snow into a sparkling jewel, with a promise of a glorious day! The horse was trotting along peacefully and perhaps daydreaming a bit too.

"Bill it is getting late, we better go a little faster," Olga said.

Bill hit Star with the tail end of the reins and just then a snowshoe rabbit jumped up and startled the horse. He shied to the side and broke the shaft. With more noise added to his wrath filled soul, Star went wild! He plunged forward at a dead run.

"Hold on everybody—it's a runaway!" Bill screamed.

He braced his feet against the front panel of the buggy and guided the horse into the school yard. The horse ran himself out by then and was shaking like a leaf. This was watched by the children and the teacher through the windows. We must have provided a bit of drama and nearly gave poor Mrs. Marsh heart failure. It caused quite a commotion in the school when we got there. They all ran out to see how we were—well, not bad, as this had happened to us before, but not coming to school. I think we enjoyed it more than Star. After checking us and realizing that only two things needed attention, she said,

"Bill put Star in the shed and you can fix the buggy during your lunch hour. It is getting late and the class must come in."

The day ended with highlights of many questions, which Bill answered—somewhat feeling like a hero. The hero of the day was feeling pretty shaky, however, by the time we got home. Bill was reprimanded by dad for being lax, but I guess they were happy to know that their tribe was safe. The day was not a total loss—the other three boys had found the stray horses.

Spring had sprung and with it had released exhilarating emotions in beast and men. This was a day of all days that was remembered for a long time by many. The morning was absolutely perfect—the sun was busy softening the snow and melting the ice. On the road to school there were many dips. This particular one was quite deep and previously filled with snow and frozen over hard—but we were able to go over it with ease. True to contrary—this morning—the horse stopped on the edge and refused to budge.

"Anyone of you want to walk across while I drive the horse around?" Jim asked.

We all got out. I was the only one that wouldn't walk across the frozen dip. I crawled under the fence and walked the long way to avoid it. The rest started across only to break through up to their arm pits. It just wasn't that warm under water. Jim called for the bunch to get into the buggy and covered them up as well as he could and drove as fast as he dared. By the time we got to school, the wet clothes started to freeze on the outside and the cold crept into the warm souls of the brave, or those with less horse sense than the horse. Mrs. Marsh was shocked at the sight, but being a person of quick recovery, she started giving orders like a sergeant.

"Jim and Lyle go get more fuel and put in the stove," she said.

At the back of the school room was a big potbelly stove. She assigned some of the older children to help with the removal of overshoes, coats and stockings, and as much else as was possible. She covered the children up with other children's coats. Their cold hands and feet were put into warm water. After much commotion, things quieted down. Steam was formed from the wet clothes. All of a sudden Mrs. Marsh noticed that I was not wet.

"Rose is the only one dry. She is smart," Mrs. Marsh said.

I was pleased at her remark. I really was a coward at heart where water was concerned—then and even to this day.

"I smell smoke, my goodness! The schoolhouse is on fire!" someone yelled.

Jim climbed into the attic and buckets of snow and water were passed up to him. Mike climbed on the roof of the schoolhouse. Before long the fire was out, children revived, dried, and class resumed, but most of all Mrs. Marsh was still standing on her two feet with all her sense—what else could she do with such lively children—but keep on her toes.

I took it upon myself to invite her to dinner that day. After asking me if my parents knew of the invitation, I responded,

"No, but they would be pleased."

Mrs. Marsh hesitantly accepted. My folks were pleased to meet her. It was not unusual for people dropping in our home without any notice beforehand. We did not have a phone except our congenial nature. My parents were very hospitable people. Mrs. Marsh seemed very relaxed and was enjoying the evening with us. We asked her to spend the night with us, but she declined.

"No—perhaps some other time. But thank you all for a lovely evening," she said.

After that Mrs. Marsh was more relaxed with us. Good thing as we learned to love her and accepted her as one of us. She was a wonderful person and teacher. We really had no problem with loving the teachers we had through the years. Looking back on our childhood days and our home life, it does not surprise me now. We were taught to obey our elders and to respect their position in life graciously—without rebellion. This does not mean that we did not have our moments of tantrums and tears, but this was corrected and eased into proper heading, as there were many classified heads with such a large family; but there were only two bosses to correct.

If there was any dispute among us children, we tried to correct each other, but never to strike at one another in anger. That was the job for our parents—to punish the guilty.

The climax of our first year of school in America ended very fortunately for all—considering the boy made trap without foresight. The morning was the start of a beautiful day—the ground had a firm frozen top. We were driven to school in the buggy. Before the day was over—the chinook took over and brought about the wind that blew the pebbles about, softening the earth and making it muddy. There were only patches of snow here and there.

Mike decided to come and pick us up on a homemade sled. He put a wagon seat on it and brought a canvas along. He hitched two horses to the sled as pulling was hard in such thawing. Since the countryside was open he was able to follow the high spots, with some snow on it yet, and the rocky barren places.

Mike was a happy-go-lucky young man, and kind. Life was a great adventure to him. This idea of transportation was a challenge to Mike. He was a handsome lad—blue eyes like Montana skies and a smile to go with it. He was the rugged outdoor type with sandy hair. He was all smiles—pulling into the school yard._

"Mike, do you think that you'll get home all right in this wind and mud?" Mrs. Marsh inquired.

"Oh, sure," he said.

We never questioned—we got onto the flat sled, about six inches off the ground, and sat down on the seat that was not secured to it. With the strong wind blowing pebbles and other small objects into our eyes, Mike threw the canvas over us and wrapped the ends around the seat. It was not the healthiest situation, as the air became very close. We were trying to get Mike's attention, but he was vocalizing at the top of his voice and did not hear us. He was lost in his own performance to the great wide world as his stage. Mike had—has a fine singing voice. You could call it a miracle, or an act of God.

A stray cat got his attention, as he was a great lover of animals. Mike stopped to pick the animal up and lifted the canvas only to throw the cat in with us, causing some air to flow in, but only for a moment, as he was afraid the cat would escape. The cat, finding itself closed in with our flying arms, was sent into frenzy. We, too, wanted out to protect ourselves from the wild flailing claws of the cat. Next thing we knew, we tumbled off the sled with the seat, cat, and all. The cat ran—I am sure—with only one thought—escape from the mad world of terror; and as for us, we too came to life—air—and freedom from suffocation with a cat. We called and called for Mike, as he was quite a ways from us before realizing that he had lost his charge. He was singing again. Finally hearing us, he turned around and came to get us very much surprised at the outcome of tears, fright and scratched children.

We refused to be covered with canvas going home the rest of the way. Mike was given a lesson by dad on how to be aware of his duties at all times, especially when he was given a responsibility involving other people's lives. He usually gave a good talking to the offender and less hand work. It seemed to have more effect without loss of dignity to the growing pains of youth.

School was out—it was vacation time—what wonderful days to look forward to. Yes, there would be work, but also picnics.

Before school was out, most of the planting had been done, like field seeding and garden planting. This of course left only pest control—which was watched daily—on the spot jobs—you could say. The bugs were all handpicked, carefully put into a can, and fuel poured over them.

Many happy times we spent on the Teton River picking berries and wading in the river. We'd take a picnic lunch along and spend most exhilarating hours.

On one of those lovely picnic outings, we took a washtub and a few lard buckets with handles to pick berries. Six of us went berry picking—Bill, Olga, Lyda, Maurice, George, and I left early in the morning for Teton River. It was a lovely day. It did not take long to fill the tub and buckets with berries and there still was plenty of time left for play. Towards evening the dark angry clouds were gathering, so we hurriedly proceeded on our way home, hoping to beat the storm. Such wrath of anger—thunder, lightning and then rain—as if heaven opened up and poured everything out at once. The bottom of the buggy filled with rainwater and the berries were floating out of their containers. We were sitting in it like a bunch of drowned mice, starry eyed, but very much alive.

Star had his usual scare and runaway—which winded him— so he was out of breath. Bill was able to keep him under control, regardless of heaven's wrath that day. When we came into the yard of our farm, the sun came out and it seemed as if the whole world was washed clean and sparkled like morning dew with the fragrance of the countryside. Mother and dad had left that morning for a visit to my brother Sam's place, which was about thirty miles from our farm. They had not returned as yet—not unusual as it took longer in those days with horse and buggy—besides they wanted to spend the day with them. We knew it would be late at night before they would return. We got busy looking over the fowl and little animals. It seemed that most of the animals had found their way into the shelter. It was a rule to leave an opening large enough for their safety in case of such unforeseen catastrophes.

The only casualty was a mother hen and her baby chicks—or so it seemed at the time. She had twenty chicks (not all of her own, for my mother figured that a loving mother should not waste her affection only on a few, so she added a few more to the kind mother hen), and we found them all lying about half way to the chicken coop. By all appearances they'd died by drowning. Olga gathered the few that still twitched a little and placed them into a large pan and put them into the oven. Olga asked me to dispose of those that were left on the ground, so I picked each one up and threw it onto a lean-to shed—attached to the main barn.

After the chores were done, Olga proceeded to start a fire in the range to make supper, as we called it at that time. She had forgotten the baby chicks she had placed in the oven earlier. In the meantime the warmth of the sun returned life back to mother hen, and just like a devoted mother, she started looking for her babies. She was waddling about the yard calling for her baby chicks. The chicks on the shed came to and heard her call. They jumped off the shed, and such a reunion could only be appreciated by someone else that had had the same experience. I am afraid we did not understand the miracle, or bothered to question it except, we were so happy to be able to tell mama that everything was fine, as the poultry-raising was her project.

While making the evening meal, Olga heard chirping coming from the oven; she opened the oven and all the chicks were jumping up and down in the pan. Some of them had burned their poor little toes. She took them out and put fresh cow's cream on their feet. After they had quieted down, she took them to their mother. By the time they all nestled under her, she was standing on her tiptoes, but she was happy—I am sure.

DOLL

My sister Raya and I had a great desire for a doll—just any kind of doll—but that would have been a luxury at that time. World War II was going strong. Everybody was making sacrifices, and we should, by all means, with such a large family.

My oldest brother Matt was quite artistic, so he proceeded to carve us a doll out of wood. The characteristics were there, but it wasn't soft to the touch. I can assure you the wooden head was loved, as much as wood could be cuddled. It lasted until all the similarities were lost. Next was mother's creation, which lasted as long as the string around the stuffed head of a blanket.

Now, with a couple of creative and bright girls like us, and then watching the so called professional at work, we came up with a most fantastic idea. We had had our eyes on our baby brother George for sometime. One bright morning it came to pass. After my sister Olga finished dressing George—following mother's orders—and left him playing on the middle of the bed—he seemed happy and contented, for he was not aware that his two darling sisters—who generally cuddled and kissed him so fondly—were planning such an unorthodox calamity.

When we came to him, he was so delighted. His hands were waving as though he were talking—his baby talk—which most of the time was deciphered under different circumstances—but this was under pressing times, and besides we couldn't look him in the face. Quickly, well, as quickly as I could with my small hands handle a big baby, I got his clothes off, while Raya gathered up the diapers, blanket, towels and whatever else we thought we would need, or could get our hands on.

Before we could leave, Olga came in to see why George was crying. Raya and I dove under the bed with our treasure. Mother followed Olga in to see what the noise was about. She began scolding Olga for not minding her right away.

"Why the baby could catch his death of cold," mama said.

"Mother, I did dress him. I just don't understand what happened," Olga replied.

"Well, dress him again!" mother said, leaving Olga in tears.

Olga was 11 years old and a beautiful girl. She had daddy's coloring, brown eyes, lovely features with chestnut, curly hair. She was a petite person. We heard that she looked like daddy's mother. Daddy was very concerned about her—that she was worked too hard by our loving mother. Mother believed that idleness bred trouble. Father voiced his concern to mother many times about it.

"You could do some of the household duties yourself and not spend so much time outside," he said.

This ruffled mother up, as she was responsible for all poultry-raising and this took a lot of her time. She had a variety of every kind. Mother enjoyed her work.

By some miracle, a baby girl-chick was hatched to a Rock Island mother hen. As the chick grew, her coloring was bluish-grey and she had a curly tuft for a crown. Now this proud chick never mingled with the rest, or ate with them. She would walk along the outside of the fence with her head up high; then she'd wait until all were through eating before she'd come back to eat.

"You'll lose that crown that you are so proud of, if you don't accept your neighbors," mother would say.

Sure enough it happened! Her beautiful plume was gone and all she had to show for it was a bloody and sore head, but did that stop her, oh, no! Well, that was more than an average chicken could take. Mother came to her rescue one early morning, but not early enough, as the young chicken was being pecked to death by half a dozen hens. Mother picked her up and brought her to the house. We were all sort of fond of "Glory"—that was her name—and we were sad for her.

"Let this be a lesson to us all. Being proud is one thing, but it can be carried too far! Being a little humble is much more to be proud of," mother said.

Perhaps this is ahead of my story, but I thought it sort of tied in with the little hen, that stood up for what she thought was right, but of course mother was right!

"You leave the girls to me. You know she is the oldest of the girls at home now and must learn the duties of housekeeping and cooking. What if something should happen to me, like illness, or even death! What would you do then?" mother reasoned.

"But she is so little," daddy said.

"Yes I know," mother said, "but she is strong and healthy."

Father left mother shaking his head. Raya and I heard mother scolding Olga and it made us sad to hear her crying, but we did want that doll! Pretty soon Olga left the room again, this time taking George with her. He was a big baby and it took tight holding to keep him from wiggling out of one's arms. Since Olga was so tiny, she had her arms full.

My, but we were tired—lying so still and trying to keep from shaking in our, so called, boots. We were barefooted, as it was good old summer time. I peeked out cautiously to see if the coast was clear. Yes, it was and we quickly crawled out from underneath the bed with our treasure and ran to the door to see if the rest of the way was clear too. We were in luck again and ran out of the house to our makeshift play house, that I had made, much against my father's wishes, out of a grain box that he had unloaded in the yard. We put boards across the top for the roof and left a small opening for the door. Raya and I even involved our brother Bill much against his better judgment in helping us with the heavy lifting.

"You know that this is not for long. Just as soon as dad finishes loading the fence posts on the flatbed and mends the fence, he'll want the box to haul grain again," Bill cautioned.

But being of pioneer stock, we were used to fleeting periods of joy and told him so. Bill was only two years older than I, and his heart was crisper than a head of a cabbage, where we were concerned. We dashed up the ladder that was leaning against the side of the grain box. We dropped the treasure in and nearly fell in ourselves.

So a couple of angels proceeded to make their dream come true. First the head was made by putting a few diapers in the middle of a diaper then drawing up that diaper and tying a string around it to hold the other diapers in place. Next the stockings were filled and pinned to the diaper that hung from the head part. The shirt went on next with sleeve ends tied and stuffed, and then the shirt was buttoned and stuffed, followed by a pair of bib pants. A babushka was put on its sweet round head with the tail ends wrapped to the back and tied. Good, heavens—a baby without a face. Raya looked at me with her big emerald eyes.

"Frasinia, it doesn't have eyes!"

She pointed to her own face and finally came to her mouth. Her finger must have tasted good, or she was weary, for she left it in her mouth. But I still had a job to complete. It must have been good for we were both jubilant with our project. I got a pencil and told Raya to look at me. She stared at me with her eyebrows up and sucking away at her fingers. I knew that when George got hungry he'd suck on his finger and mother would say,

"The baby is hungry!"

So I decided Raya needed food. I told her to stay there and I'd go to the house and get us some food. That's where I made the mistake. Olga cornered me to dry the dishes as that was one of my duties. I begged Olga to let me take some food to Raya first. She let me go after the dishes were done. I ran back to Raya and our doll. It looked almost human.

I gave the doll to Raya, since she always played the part of mother and me the papa. The doll was too much for either one of us, so we took turns carrying it. What a joyous time we had, but again short-lived, as wash day came and missing clothes had to be found. Of course we did not know that Jim was informed by Olga what happened when he found her in tears. Jim was on a lookout for the guilty culprits.

Unwary that the night sky was falling, we happily walked around the farmyard with our creation, laughing and chattering childish prattle—making plans for a trip to town. Daddy had a big box sitting by the side of the bunkhouse and that was our pretend carriage to drive into town.

"So you're the ones!" Jim said.

He snatched the doll out of Raya's arms and right before our eyes, he dismantled it, which startled us to earth from the rosy clouds of dreams. Raya and I begged Jim not to do it. We were crying with uncontrolled sobs. Father came up on the scene. He was angry at such tactics with little children, or anyone else, and not in so many words expressed it to Jim. After all, he was seventeen years old and should have known better. Jim was feeling badly, I am sure.

"Pick up those clothes and take them to mother!" daddy said.

Daddy took us into his arms and quieted us down with a promise of a doll. We showed our appreciation, as any little daughters would. These emotional times always left daddy dewy eyed, but our world was righted again. Sure enough we got our promised doll a few weeks later. She wasn't very big, but had pretty blue eyes and blonde hair. Now, none of us girls had blue eyes, so the doll must have reminded daddy of mama, as she was the blue eyed gal in the family.

PAINTING

Painting pictures and drawing were natural talents that seemed to emerge early. One of the earliest experiences I recall involved drawing eyes on the face of the homemade doll Raya and I made from diapers and clothes we took off of our baby brother George. Although my hand-drawn face on that homemade doll was short-lived—as the borrowed diapers and clothes were missed and needed—my talent for drawing continued to evolve.

Later on painting was added to my repertoire of artistic skills, and through the years, all were developed further when I received guidance and instruction from professional artists conducting the various painting classes I took. Painting was an escape and a relaxation for me. While I was painting, problems of the day disappeared.

I have always been inspired by the beauty of life and the landscape around me, no matter where I lived, and I drew upon these memories and motivations to create works on paper and canvas. I've painted numerous landscapes, seascapes, flowers, animals, and birds, using the mediums of oil and watercolor, and I am happy to say that many family members and friends have my paintings gracing the walls in their homes.

LITTLE MOTHERS

When George was fifteen months, mother and father informed us children one evening after a nice meal that they had to go into Great Falls, Montana, to do their annual shopping for the winter months and buy clothes for school and for the rest of the family. Mother and dad looked forward to these outings after long months of work and devotion to their tribe. Since it was so far, it usually took all of two weeks—especially with horse and wagon.

Now, what brought on this trip wasn't just the usual shopping alone, we learned later that mother helped deliver a baby, her grandson, a new nephew for us, a son for our oldest brother Matt and his wife Paraska. Mother was and had been a midwife in her village in Russia for years. She even told me later in my life how she used the husband's or some other handy lap to help deliver the baby, if the delivery was a problem. The expectant mother would straddle on her husbands slightly spread lap to help quicken or ease the natural birth. Most of the births were taken care of by midwives, or some handy neighbor, or could even be a lonely traveler stopping for a drink of water or direction in some lonely out of the way place.

Oh, goodness, I am getting ahead of myself—now going back to the morning before the folks left. Orders were given to all, since Olga was the oldest of the girls at home and Jim of the boys. Jim took his orders seriously. As for Olga, she was more for asking if we'd help her. Baby George was in the weaning period when mother and dad were leaving on their trip.

"Mother what should I do if George should start missing you?" Olga asked.

"Just give him milk from the glass, mother said.

Dad did better than that. He spoke with a neighbor—a couple that had lost a baby two weeks previously and had a mutual understanding that they would check on the family, and particularly the baby's welfare. She was delighted to be of any help and most of all to feel the baby in her arms. What an armful. He covered me when Olga placed him in my lap.

It seemed that George realized his loving mother was gone. He would not eat or drink from the cup. Now, Olga came up with a good solution, so she thought. She took a catsup bottle and a nipple that we used to feed the lambs. She washed them the best she knew how and proceeded to fill the bottle with milk and put on the finishing touch, the nipple.

"Frasinia, hold George in your lap and try to feed him. I have to fix supper," Olga said.

Now, as I said before, George was an armful just to hold onto with both of my arms around him. I had one thing going for me, he was hungry and the nipple spurred him on to grab the bottle with both hands and to his surprise it was more than he ever had before.

"Olga, Olga—George is swallowing the nipple!" I screamed.

She rushed over and pulled the nipple out of his mouth, as the milk was spilling over me. Poor little fellow had the scare of his life. Boy if that wouldn't wean a baby—but no! He just screamed bitterly at such indignation. Of course, how was he to know of our good intention? Just as if a good angel gave the message at that precise moment the dear neighbors walked in. They came to see how we were managing, but most of all—the baby. When the neighbor realized what transpired, she begged us to let her take George home with her and promised to take good care of him until the folks came home.

"Oh, no," we voiced as one. "We promised the folks we'd take care of him."

The neighbor lady realized that it was to no avail to beg, so she bathed George and nursed him. Putting his broken world together again, he relaxed to her soft voice and sweet smile and finally fell into blissful sleep. She asked us to promise to call them no matter what time of the day or night it might happen that she was needed. She promised to be back in the morning and check on George's needs.

Olga was relieved of great responsibility and expressed her thanks to Mrs. Olson. Brother Jim expressed his gratitude also. Olga was so young for such responsibility, but that was not questioned then—after all there were older ones in the family to fall back on for help. As for George, he must have been in seventh heaven.

After two weeks of our parents' absence, the reunion was joyous—then came gifts of clothes and other goodies to eat—things we didn't have all the time—well, like fresh fruit, candy and gum.

We were told that a new bouncing son was born to our brother Matt and his wife Paraska. While there the folks saw many foreign speaking friends which made their trip a joyous one.

The days fell into a normal schedule once again, well, as much as possible, as life does have a way of sneaking in a twist of surprises. Spring came with all its glory and refreshing, fragrant, perfumed air—ah—such a morning—what a wonderful gift to share. It was too good to last—and just as Raya and I decided to give a spring cleaning to the bunk house for the boys, without orders from higher authority.

Now, George was an adventuresome child—his walks brought him to most unexpected calamities, poor baby. Like the spring cleaning day, oh, my, Raya and I were just pushing the cold potbelly stove from the middle of the room, when our darling brother walked in front as the stove was falling over. His scream frightened us. We screamed for mother. As she rushed in, we ran out. Cowards! No—just frightened out of our wits.

Raya and I were scared as to what happened and wondered if George was badly hurt. We would cry and then ask God to forgive us. If only he would make George well, we promised never to do it again—spring cleaning. We lay on the side of a knoll back of the barn, as the evening shadows started to creep and the coyotes started their calls.

"They'll feel badly if the coyotes get us," I said.

We started running towards the house, as we were afraid of our own shadows. Slamming the door behind us, all eyes were on us. Then we saw George walking towards us. We were so happy to see him well that we forgot our own problem. We were caressing him as mother walked up and said,

"You two are lucky that the stove just barely grazed him. We knew where you were all the time, and I hope this will be a lesson to you both."

"Oh, mama, it is—it is!" we both chimed.

Stranger than fiction, the folks had ideas of their own kind of punishment, as we had been missing all day and had had no lunch, besides dad and mother gave us a good talking to. We promised never to take things into our own hands without consulting them first. It seems some have to go through life serving the traps while others make their own traps in life to hurdle.

GOLD DUST TWINS

Raya and I were like a couple of gold dust twins. If you were looking for one, you'd find the other one. Late in the evening after dinner was over, a horse and buggy pulled into the yard. It had been snowing all day and was very cold. We were looking through the window where we had cleared enough frost to peek.

"Oh, mama, someone is coming to the house. It is a lady and a man," we both chimed at the same time.

She went to the door and let the couple in. They asked if it was possible to stay overnight as they were lost and hungry.

"Yes!" mama said.

Then she noticed that the woman was pregnant and that her clothes were wet. The man and my father went out to take care of the horse. Mother had the woman change her clothes into some of hers and put her on the nice heated brick bed that was part of mama's cooking stove. Mother had forgotten about us two and we were taking this all in. All of a sudden mother noticed us and told us go to bed. The lady smiled at us. She realized we had never seen a big tummy before, from the expression on our faces.

The next morning after breakfast the couple was preparing to leave. The husband brought in a little paper carton and gave it to his wife. She got a fork from mother and started eating something that looked like white skinned mice to us. She offered some to Raya and me.

"We don't like mice," we told her.

"These are not mice—they're Oysters. I wanted some and my husband got them for me," she said laughing.

"I know how it feels to crave for unusual food," mother said and smiled.

Father gave them the right direction and they left on their way which wasn't very far from our place.

One night I had to get up to go to the bathroom, which was outside, and I did not know that the folks had a late visitor who was spending the night and was laid to sleep right by the kitchen range on the floor close to the door to go outside. I nearly stepped on him—just at the time I noticed his eyes looking up at me. I rerouted my step and went outside. I noticed his back was turned to the stove when I came back inside. Cold air came in with me and I was chilly so my only thought was to crawl back into a warm bed. If there were others with the same nature call, the poor man must have had a cold head. Anyway he was gone before I got up the next morning.

Since daddy was the early riser, he kept a shovel handy by the house to pick up the calling cards of the night visitors, as he knew his tribe wouldn't go any further than a few steps around the house when it was so cold. Many times when young cowboys would drop in to see us, or stay over night, and if their Levis were torn, mama would make them put on someone's pants that fit and mend theirs. They knew better than to object. She got many thanks from strangers and people they knew. Mama would knit each one in the family a pair of wool stockings for winter. Oh, yes, and mittens. Of course if they were not worn out they were handed down to the younger ones. Many times she re-knitted the worn places, as the tops didn't wear out as quickly.

One day Raya and I crawled into the wheat bin and pretended we were swimming. We were really having fun when Mama's voice reached our ears. We tried to scramble out fast but the wheat was moving faster. This was a forbidden place to lie in as it was dangerous. Mama came in and heard us mumbling. She helped us out and pulled our braids for not minding her. While we were trying to get out, I caught my arm on a nail and broke through the skin. Well, my arm was bleeding, as we were marched into the house in front of mama. We had to spend the rest of the time in the house. Raya noticed my arm and asked me if I were going to die.

"Oh no, but it would sure make mama feel bad if I did," I said.

"Frasinia, come here!" mama called.

She cleaned my cut, put some brown powder on it, and tied a clean cloth around it.

"Now you two better not think you can outthink me," mama said.

RAYA'S RED SHOES

What a joy it was for Raya when daddy came home from town one day and handed her a package to open! She hardly could contain herself before she opened it. Her eyes grew bigger by the minute. Daddy helped her to put on the red shoes—such a proud little girl. Daddy got a big hug and a kiss from his little daughter. But that wasn't all—a toy wrist watch too—which was put on her wrist. My, my, this was Raya's big day!! We all admired it over and over throughout the day.

Raya's presents laid lovingly by her side that night while she slept. Having admiration from all her brothers and sisters was not enough, she strolled in the yard for all the fowl and animals to see, and she wandered into the cow corral to show her pretty shoes—but to her fatal sorry. Her red shoes turned brown. Daddy was in there throwing in fresh straw so the cattle could bed down at night. Raya was crying from the horror of it all, when daddy lifted her out of the cattle mire. Of course her shoes were ruined and short-lived.

I remembered her next pair of shoes was of the same style but black patent leather. She wore them with more discretion. Mother would see her carrying them in her hands more often than on her feet, if she was wandering anywhere in the yard.

LAMBING

Spring had sprung and lambing time arrived. Father did not raise sheep, but it seemed the good neighbor's eves gave birth to twins that spring—lucky us. Orphaned lambs were called bums. Well, we got thirty such bums. This involved quite a feeding problem. They had to be bottle fed. Catsup bottles were used. For once there were more lambs than children. Sister Olga filled five bottles with milk and assigned each one of us little busy bodies to feed the thirty little bums.

"How do we know when the lambs had enough milk?" I asked Olga.

"If the lamb's tummy puffs out, it had enough; then take it away and give it to another one," she answered.

While this information was given out, my darling baby brother George (now known as George Montgomery) got hold of one of the bottles and started feeding the lambs. This really started a riot between the lambs—each one wanted to be first at the bottle.

Well, you can guess who had the worst! George's ears, toes (as he was barefooted) and fingers were sucked on. The bottle was on the ground with one lamb down on his knees wagging his tail—enjoying his undisturbed meal. George was screaming and crying at the top of his voice for help. (He was only three.) We all ran to his rescue. He turned out just fine with all his digits quite normal and no lamb complex. He avoided them for a while, with a purple passion, but only for a while, as they became good friends later when grass became their diet.

PET EAGLE

We got another addition to our pet department— an eagle. Maurice and Bill went hunting one Saturday morning and came home with a baby eagle. It seems while mama and papa eagles were gone—our brothers climbed the height to the home of the eagles and took their baby. They had to keep it penned up for awhile. After a few weeks they brought it out and let it loose in the yard. It became quite tame, but it never lost its wild delight in getting its own fresh dinner.

Mama started missing her baby chicks. So she caught the culprit in action one day. He just walked up to a chick and helped himself. Well, he just had to go! The boys pleaded, but to no avail. The boys took Baldy's picture and without too many tears, Baldy was returned to his home. We used to see a couple eagles flying over our farm and wondered if they were Baldy's parents.

BLACK STALLION

Going on our last picnic before school started was an experience, which still remains vivid in my mind to this day. Of all the places we picnicked, this was the loveliest place. We all agreed. There was a beautiful spring—water bubbling up, a few trees and tall green grass. We no sooner settled to enjoy our nourishing spread of food, we brought along, when we heard hoof beats and such snorting, as only an angry horse makes. Lucky for us there was a fence about fifty feet away. We didn't stop to pick the food up; we just ran for the fence as fast as we could. I had George by the hand—poor darling—he was more dragged than running.

As we came to the fence, we dropped to the ground—rolling underneath to the other side. I rolled George ahead of me. After we got some distance away, we turned to look at our foe. It was a beautiful black stallion and his harem. We had trespassed on his sacred place—"Heaven forbid." He was pawing the earth and shaking his head—making noises at us. You can rest assured we didn't invade his home again.

It was not long after that, that my brother Maurice had a heartbreaking experience. He was only five years old at the time. During one of his visits to see our neighbor Steve Sevacheko, Maurice was chased by none other than the beautiful black stallion—with a long memory—or so it seemed. Steve was out in his yard and could see a great distance, as the countryside was quite flat and he could see what was taking place. He opened the gate to his yard.

Maurice was riding bareback—holding on for dear life to the reins and mane of the horse (Pacer). Maurice and the horse entered in a dead run while Steve closed the gate. Steve brought Maurice home that evening with horse and wagon—leaving Pacer, trailing behind, tied to the wagon. Steve told mama and daddy of Maurice's horrible experience.

"I had quite a time getting his fingers untangled from the reins and the mane. He could've been killed," Steve said.

This ended Maurice's lone rides and our picnics without supervision.

GEORGE'S LITTLE LAMB

This Little Lamb came to live on a big mixed up farm. His mama had three little lambs and could not take care of them all by herself, so her master gave one to George's daddy. When George saw the little lamb he fell in love with it. George was not quite three years old. His daddy saw a need for a pet for his little son. Besides the little lamb would get the love it needed now.

"All right George, this is your little lamb," daddy said.

"You'll have to feed him with milk from a bottle."

George was so happy he hugged the little lamb close to him.

"Oh, thank you, daddy, thank you," and he kissed his daddy on the check.

"I will be so good to the little lamb and do everything you say, daddy."

In a short time little lamb was happy—because he had someone that loved him. It was not long before the little lamb and George went on walks around the big mixed up farm. George told everyone that little lamb was his friend. Of course they looked up and made polite noises.

One day when they were out on their walk, George bent over to pat the little lamb! Goodness—George's nose was close to little lamb's mouth and he started to suck on it. Little lamb must have thought it was a nipple. This frightened George; he ran home to his mama crying.

"What is the matter George? My poor baby," she said.

"I will never play with little lamb again. He sucked my nose," George said—while feeling to see if his nose was still there.

"Oh, I am sure little lamb did not mean to hurt you," mama said.

Next morning the little lamb came by to go for a walk with George. George was hiding back of his mama and would not go with the little lamb. The little lamb went away so sad. Then mama got a wonderful idea. Why not teach little lamb to drink from a pail and have George help her.

At first George was afraid, but mama was right there, so he became brave and held the pail while the little lamb was learning to drink from it. The little lamb would wag his tail while drinking the milk. George thought that was so funny he laughed with delight.

Mama was very pleased with the outcome of her idea. She heard George ask the little lamb if he was tired one day. The little lamb rubbed his nose on George's coveralls. What friends they were becoming.

When little lamb learned to drink out of the pail and nibble the green grass, George forgave the little lamb for what he did to his nose, and they started going out for long walks again. The little lamb would stop to eat the green grass. George enjoyed doing summersaults while waiting for little lamb. When they got tired they would lie down on the green grass to rest.

FORTY DAYS OF LENT

Easter was one sacred holiday that was observed with humble enthusiasm. For forty days the whole family observed lent—except a nursing baby. Now this lent was not one of these just denying oneself of one or two things, but the whole family religiously and faithfully would eat no meat of any kind, or dairy products. We were the closest to being vegetarian than a vegetarian himself. No questions were asked why such strong rules; they were accepted cheerfully.

Then came the day of preparation for Easter day—this made up for all the days of lent. We were taught the meaning of the day—such joy it was—like being reborn again into a new world. The house was washed inside and out. As Easter comes in the spring, so do the flowers. We gathered the spring flowers and mixed them with new green grass and with some clean straw. This would be sprinkled all over the floor.

By the evening of Good Friday, everything had to be done. A dish of cooked wheat, Paska, and prunes were placed in front of the Holy Family. The mixture of straw, grass and flowers were put under the dish first. In the pot of freshly growing green wheat blades, about four or six colored eggs were placed and put on the table. This growth of wheat was planted a few weeks ahead, as a prediction whether the year will be bountiful, or poor. Well, the pot was full of green wheat— a very promising year. It was good to live with such faith from day to day; at least faith brought strength to meet the unforeseen. At least a hundred eggs were colored, as we were a large family—besides there were always people dropping in.

Easter bread (Paska) was baked. Such fragrant aroma and so delicious—one must taste it to appreciate the unusual goodness. I recall we had plenty of fresh apples, or oranges at times, but mostly dried fruit—prunes, raisins, pears, peaches, and apricots—which would grace our table on Easter Day.

Mother would cook some of the dry fruit together—my how we looked forward to it. Daddy's favorite dish was prepared too—prunes and beef cooked together, very tasty I must say. A whole pot of whole wheat grain was cooked in clear water. Then honey was diluted in hot water and poured over it after portions were dished out to us on Easter morning. The taste is delicious with a nut like flavor, although one must acquire the taste for such food to appreciate it as the nutritious gift from God to mankind.

In the east side corner of the living room, mother had what was considered a kneeling place to say our prayers. She had a picture of the Holy Family—Joseph, Mary and child. A lace cloth was covering the corner table and lace curtains hung from the ceiling with tie backs. The candle, placed in front of the picture, was lit early morning and evening during prayer times.

It was not unusual to see someone crossing themselves anytime during the day. As many as there were of us—there were times when help was needed, or advice from some one higher-up.

Now, on Good Friday, the mixture of spring flowers, green grass and clean straw was placed on the holy table with a small pot of cooked wheat—colored eggs around the pot—prunes, or mixture of cooked fruit and Paska.

This was our starter for Easter breakfast. During the night it was blessed by the Holy Family—beautiful faith. The reflection on the Holy Family's faces was beautiful—illuminated by the lit candle which was left burning all night.

All the food was prepared for the week of Easter—so as not to sin on Sabbath days—Borscht, breads, roast, pork, or turkey and Piroshki. Easter morning, we all got up at sunrise to greet the Holy Day. We went to the bowl of colored eggs and picked a red egg—which we washed our faces with in cold water. We were told we'd get pink cheeks. Well—we did; but now I believe it was from the cold water, that we had to break the thin layer of ice on, at least the first one there did.

This was one of the days when we all showed affection towards each other. We would exchange colored eggs and kiss. We all got down on our knees and said a prayer after our father, even the baby was held in mother's arms and helped to cross itself.

The breakfast was started with the blessed piece of Easter bread (Paska), that mother brought from Russia with her, which had been blessed in the church while they were there. As it was slowly disappearing—a very small portion of crumbs was given to each one with a glass of grape juice to wash it down. After that we could eat just anything we desired, or should say whatever we had on the table.

After breakfast, the prayers of thank you to God were said. Everybody pitched in to help clear the table and help with washing the dishes. The food was left on the table and covered with a table cloth. This was one of times that the neighbors would try and see each other, as the distance was great with only horse and buggy, or a wagon for transportation. We seemed to have our share of neighborly visits. It was a joy to see them. Of course our table was always full and open to company.

There were other rare occasions when a traveling minister would come to our schoolhouse and this would bring the people from far corners to hear the good word. Being it was a long day the folks brought their food with them and it usually turned into a picnic, so I am sure the minister left with a warm tummy. (This was a rare communication with the minister, or the church, as most religious teachings were taught in the home by the parents.) In a short time it looked like a small town had sprung up.

HIGH HEEL SHOES

Although I was only eight years old, my greatest ambition was to wear my sister's red high heel shoes.

One Sunday morning we were preparing to attend church services. I spied my heart's desire—high heel shoes. Since my sister was not home, I was sure she'd never know they were used. I tried them on, but they just dropped off my feet. Well, if I kept my toes curled up, the shoes would stay on and I would be able to walk like my big sister.

I was not unnoticed for long. As we were going into the schoolhouse where the services were to be held, a little boy stared at my shoes. Gliding slyly towards me with a mischievous grin, he said,

"Oh, you have your big sister's shoes on."

With fear in my heart, I put my finger to my lips to hush him up and glanced at my mother. Thank goodness she was busy talking—I thought. At the most impressive part of the service, my toes uncurled. Plop! The shoes fell off. The look I received from my mother could have curled my toes again.

THE PRIZE RAM

The bully of the farm was our prize ram. It must have gone to his head—big curly horns and beautiful white wool coat. He would always strut around the farmyard like some Monarch, but this made very little impression on us children.

Bill made a wagon. He used the wheels off of our play wagon and built a deep square wooden box on it. Oh, yes, Bully had a harness made to fit him too. Bill would hitch Bully to the wagon. Olga and Bill would get into the wagon and away they'd go. Bully didn't like it very much, as it did not help his dignity any. He would make so much fuss, like kicking in the front of the box. This would only give Olga and Bill that daring excitement of living dangerously. They would drive into the yard like a couple of conquerors. As for Bully, he'd end up marching back home with grace, that would do justice to any royalty. Now, really there wasn't much else he could do. As I recall, Olga was the only brave one to ride with Bill. I was not a brave soul for such an excursion.

Dad and mother were very much against such disgraceful abuse of Bully, which before long was stopped. This did not help us children any, as Bully got pretty brave and we had to dodge him, or run for our lives to some quick exit, or we'd be battered by his horns.

The folks realized that this would never do. Dad was more sympathetic where we children were concerned; not that mother didn't love us, after all we knew she prayed each day for our health and safety—that should prove of her great devotion and concern for her family. She even added total strangers in her prayers—because she said when she closed her eyes to sleep, they all came rolling at her from all corners of the room beaming and that way she knew God heard her prayers.

One day, I stood watching mother milk the cow (Bluee), who would not let anyone else milk her unless they wore the jacket that mother used when milking—if she should happen not to be at home. Bluee would turn around and sniff at it and relax. Guess mother had that special touch that Bluee liked.

Old Bully was watching with that daring look in his eyes across to the other side in the cow barn. Mother was deep in thought, or prayer, and Bluee was chewing her cud contentedly. Mother was just about finished milking when Bully rammed into her arm. Everything seemed to go wild—the cow jumped—the milk went over and so did mother. Mother got up with her fist doubled up and started for Bully scolding him unmercifully.

"I'll teach you to go about hitting people," she said.

Well, there were few choice words in Russian, that best not be said, but that really had some effect on Bully, as he backed away from mother into the opposite wall of the barn and sat down on his hind hunches—his eyes went wild, and just then mother hit him right between his eyes.

Bully said, "Baa-a-a!"

Mother went back to calm Bluee down and to finish milking. You can rest assured Bluee had more faith in mother; and as for Bully, well, he walked wide of mother from then on. Dad was all out to get rid of Bully, but mother was still determined to keep him.

"Just look at your arm. It's all black and blue; besides he may harm one of the little ones," dad said.

"I don't think he'll bother anyone now," mother said.

She was wrong. Bully nearly battered the door in on the little house—back of the big house—with Olga in it. This really cooked the goose!! Dad decided then and there we could live nicely without Bully. After all he was raising cattle, and sheep were an added attraction and for a change of menu.

Bully was sold to a sheep rancher for a good price, even knowing his bad habits. He told dad, that Bully did not have enough to occupy himself and that is why he behaved like he did.

"I have enough for him to do that will convert his spirits to different channels," the sheep rancher said.

Bully was missed for awhile, but there were always some others, that seemed to want to challenge their wits with us.

Brother George decided to take a stroll this particular morning. Being a nature lover, he was busy patting whatever would let him. (He was not quite three years old) He picked up a baby gosling. That brought the parents on the scene. George ran for the house and in his rush ran up the cellar door with the old gander after him. By that time, George was screaming, as the old gander was beating him with his wings. What a trauma for a small child, before someone ran up and drove away the culprit.

The old gander was always hissing at us when we would get too close to his kind. Mother would lock him up when we would take the goslings out to feed in the green fields. They were such a chore to keep in line, as sometimes they would decide to chase a bug. We had a stick with a long light rope tied to it to help us try to keep them in a group, but sometimes the rope would wrap around their neck and it would be an uncomfortable situation for the gosling and the goose girl—such trials and tribulation for men and beasts.

We had a big stick laying right by the door to use, when we stepped outside, against the so-called domesticated beasts, or it could be, that they felt great need to protect themselves??

LOOKOUT TOWER

This was my field and greatly enjoyed. Our big red barn was the tower. I climbed that at least three or four times a day to see where the cattle and horses were, or if anyone was coming. The most interesting sight was to watch the great blue sky and its many—wonders. Our fine feathered friends circled about on a lookout, too, for a juicy morsel or a place to nest. If it was a nice sunny day, there were beautiful fluffy clouds floating about in the spacious wonder. Of course there were days when the sky was filled with black raging clouds that would spat their wrath onto the good earth with a display of fire works. Those were the days when I didn't linger on the lookout tower.

You'll probably wonder how we got to the top. Well, dad had a lean-to built alongside of the barn for his catch-all (water cistern, tools, sacks of grain, etc.) with a ladder leaning on the side of the lean-to. After we get on top of that, it was easy to run on the slanted roof, and then—there was another ladder nailed to the barn which was simple to climb. Once on the barn—another ladder was nailed to the roof. Simple, huh! At least it seemed easy for the young and daring youth, as I recall climbing it when I was six years old. Once up there we would look around to see if the cattle were straying out in other people's fields, or running away. If it were so, one of the brothers would get on a horse and bring them back to their fold—happy, or not, with their plans.

Now this lookout tower was not always used for legitimate purpose. There were times when the folks went to town and were gone all day. This was our day to hold a rodeo, if the weather permitted. The boys would bring in young steers and calves. We all took turns riding them. My! My! We did not always land in the most desirable places. No wonder a lookout tower was needed! The folks warned the older ones about being unkind to animals that were young, not to mention the messy clean up.

Since I had little fear of heights and loved climbing, I was assigned to the lookout tower quite often. Towards evening when I'd see our parents coming, I'd call down that the folks were coming. It usually was about the time when the cows were to be milked. If there was ever quick thinking with precision, it was then, like the turning of a page. The milk cows were put into their stalls and rodeo stock turned out into the pasture. Being that our farm was fenced in and grain fields fenced in from the pasture, it was no problem to make a big change, besides the animals were so happy to get away from it all. They ran instead of walked.

Everybody had their duties to perform and no one made an issue of it—after all—the forbidden joys were had by all. It really wasn't that we were not forbidden to have a rodeo; it was the choice of steers and calves we rode. It was stressed most strongly against such practice. The boys put up the fact that horses were broken and ridden each day—so what was the big deal!

Dad in no uncertain terms came out on top. Not for one moment did we fool the folks. But when they saw that everything was in smooth running order and no one was hurt—children, or beasts—what can one say. We would be told not to rodeo when they left on one of their trips—sometimes for all day or for a couple weeks, like times when they would go to Great Falls, Montana. (They expected one of us to report if the order was not carried out.) Great Falls was over one hundred miles from where we lived.

As Matt and his family lived there now, the folks would stay with them while they shopped and still found time to visit with a few Russian people they knew. My, they certainly were entitled to a reprieve after months of confinement with their brood—"Bless them!"

SHEP'S MANY TRAITS

Shep was a faithful Collie dog on this mixed up farm. He was a faithful servant in time of need. Daddy would sic him out early in the morning to bring in the milk cows that were in the enclosed pasture close by the farm. His orders were to be gentle; well, it depended on the mood of the cows and Shep. Sometimes the cows resented the disturbance during their tender dewy breakfast and would kick their heels up in hopes of getting Shep, but he was wise to their tricks. He would nip their heels and home they came. Some came home peacefully to be milked and to the nice treat of food that was given them. Being nipped on the heels did not help the cows dignity, so they would turn on him, but he'd get around that, and the cows would have to give up and head for home with bugged out look and snorting sounds, promising themselves they would get that dog yet!

Cows were not the only job Shep had. Horses had to be brought into the corral for field work in the spring and summer months. The horses enjoyed the challenge that Shep presented to them; it was quite an exhibition to watch. The horses would be on a lookout for Shep, lining up along the fence ready for take off. Shep was wise to their game. He would run swiftly up to them and they would take off and make two or three dead runs around the closed in area. All of a sudden they would step to look for him and he'd be standing there watching them. Then he'd round them up and head them for the corral gate that was held open by some member of the family. Oh, Shep was respected and praised; even the horses looked at him neighing and shaking their heads.

Another of Shep's good deeds was to help me catch chickens. He was "Johnny on the spot" to help. All I had to do was point to a chicken; he would walk up and put his paw on it; and I would go and get it. This did not seem to frighten the rest too much. They were used to seeing different maneuvers throughout the day, so what if one or more of their kind was picked up—it happened very often.

Chicken was one of our favorite meats. If we tried catching the chickens ourselves, then that is when the great confusion and excitement happened. It would seem as if they were enjoying the game of try and catch me if you can. During harvesting time we'd have as many as six or eight chickens to prepare for one meal. It depended on the size of the chicken.

MR. TURKEY

It was a beautiful crisp autumn day on the farm fifteen miles east of Brady, Montana, where we lived and enjoyed the many blessings from day to day, but on this day just what I had heard was really a blessing.

Now on this variety farm there were many things, but not modern facilities and an outside restroom was one of them. (I am not really getting away from the main part of the story—it all ties in.) What— no running water? And this outhouse was almost half a block away from the house, so to get there took some fast running to beat this turkey. He seemed to take this particular time to show off, or portrait his authority. He must have enjoyed the competition with us humans. I can't say it was a healthy or a normal thing to grow up with a stick in one's hand.

My, my, this turkey got over zealous on this lovely day. Several times I'd heard dad say that the turkey had to go. I could not believe my ears; why now, of all the times we wished he'd go to sleep and forget to wake-up or the folks would sell him to some other home where he'd find things going less his way. The turkey must have forgotten mother's position on this farm—too bad—so I thought how many times have we just made it into the house and slammed the door in this turkey's face only to hear his wings beating against the door. After a bit, he'd walk away with a red face making such noise that was heard by all. What a let down to his dignity.

"This turkey's got to go!"

I again heard father say to mother a few days before Thanksgiving Day. Mother was quite reluctant at first, but agreed, that this turkey was carrying his authority just too far. What his ideas were, were of no interest to the family by this time.

What brought on this sudden decision must have been that mother found herself in a much undignified position and held at bay by this turkey, challenging her to authority-ship. She was lucky dad was on hand to help. How lucky can one be? As a rule, mother was the one that walked with a soft stick (her voice) where things were concerned.

"I thought of keeping him for another year," mother said.

"There are a few other young sprouts that can carry on his field of work by spring," father said.

"Well, I hope not trying to run our family," mother said laughing.

"You know he has been doing this for sometime with the children," father said.

"I'm quite aware of all this too, so I've cautioned them to carry a stick with them," mother said.

"I saw Frasinia coming to Raya's rescue the other day when Raya was in the restroom. Lucky, Frasinia had a club with her. Can you imagine—the turkey just shook his head and strutted away—the big show off!" father said.

"The most interesting show I had the other day was to vision a race between Maurice and this turkey," father continued. "Why Maurice was actually challenging the turkey to a race, much to this turkey's confusion. The turkey gave up with a sudden stop!"

"It must have been quite a loss of dignity to this proud Casanova," mother said.

"Not really," father said. "He'll have the honor of holding up his prestige on Thanksgiving Day."

So this turkey and a tender suckling pig with all the trimmings graced our table, with all the family and a few neighborly neighbors present on that "Thanksgiving Day."

TORNADO

My first experience to be near the tornado—a whirling funnel of horror—was memorable! I was a babysitter for my brother Arrsum and his wife Liza, as he called her, but her given name was Elizabeth, who was expecting a baby. They were such a lovey dovey couple and still were. They had lost a daughter, older than Lenna and Olga, their third child. Lenna was four years old and Olga two. I was eight years old at the time and quite in demand for babysitting, but I think an older companion was more like it, besides I was handy to chase the cows out of the yard if they should wander in or go after them when milking time came.

I had been with my brother's family since school was out, and today mother was coming to take me home. School was going to start in a week. I was looking forward to going home and seeing my other brothers and sisters. When mother arrived she called out,

"Liza, there is a storm heading this way; we must hurry and go down into the basement, now!"

My brother Arrsum was out in the field plowing summer fallow about ten miles from his homestead where he had leased extra acreage. Liza hurriedly got us children down into the basement, and then she and mother followed down too. There was a small window in the basement and we all looked towards it. I looked down and saw my mother on her knees with bowed head praying; then she crossed herself and the building.

Just then there was a terrible noise and a black funnel was going right past the window! The house just shook. Then we heard a terrible crash!! It hit the big barn. There was only kindling left. A few chickens were killed. Since the cattle and horses were out in the pasture, none were hurt.

POWER OF FAITH

One early summer day mother started out on her monthly trip to Brady, Montana, to shop. This trip always called upon an early start— like before sunrise. Mother took Maurice, George and two grandsons, Jack and George, along to town. The boys very much enjoyed being able to go along, as it was a rare occasion for grownups to take along children. The trips were usually day trips by horse and buggy. Fifteen miles doesn't seem any distance now, but such a distance was different those days.

Daddy had the horse and buggy all ready for mother and the boys, with a word of caution to mother—

"Be careful and watch out, as you have taken on quite a handful with four lively boys. You'll have to have eyes in the back of your head as well."

"Oh, we shall be all right" she said.

"Be good boys and mind your mother and grandmother," dad said.

"Oh, we will; we will," they called out in unison. "Goodbye!"

This was the buggy that was always used for light traveling. One seat and the rest a box like a pickup would have. Anyway, that is where the boys sat huddled together in the bottom. They were so close to the same age that their thoughts ran in the same channel—mischief. Going to town was uneventful, as it was early, but the children, like butterflies, had to have time to stretch their wings.

When mother came home, the sun was just setting behind the big cow shed—I couldn't say mountain, or big hill, as it was in an area of rolling plains. She carried George into the house in her arms. He was pale and whimpering. She said that on the way home she felt the buggy go over something, but thinking it was a rock, she did not stop to see, as the boys had been unusually noisy coming home.

She more or less had blocked them out of her mind and did not realize they were screaming at her—screaming that George had fallen out of the wagon and she had run over him. I need not remind you again that mother had supreme faith in God's healing, and that is exactly what happened.

She laid George on the bed. She chewed together bread and onion and put the mixture on his navel, which she then covered with a cloth, as that was the area where the specks of blood came through. Next mother covered George with a quilt and said a prayer. She left me with instructions to call if George should start crying. She had to go milk the cow (Bluee) that only mother could milk.

All this time, I was standing by crying silently for George, as he looked like he would not last the night. Father came and looked at George. He seemed distressed by his appearance. Just then, mother returned and assured father that all would be well. I think father was in awe of mother. Well, at times—just at a loss for words. George was up the next morning and had a hearty breakfast. His activity was held down for a few days which helped his quick recovery with God's help.

Shortly after that Arrsum came home, frightened out of his wits for his family, as he saw the tornado coming from the direction of his homestead. He was greatly relieved to find that all was well with Liza, mother, and the children. The barn was a total loss—rough when money was so scarce. This happened shortly after World War I.

We spent the night there, and the next morning after breakfast, we started out for home. On the way home the countryside showed few places damaged, since the farms were far and few in between.

Funny, I don't recall being frightened. Mother was there and that made the world right. I can't recall her getting panicked; it seemed she was the strongest when trauma was about. She would place things into God's hands and went about her work. Dad was pretty much like that too.

Mother was greatly relieved that our place was intact. The tornado seemed to have skirted its way across the country, and whatever was in its way, it destroyed. The family got together to help rebuild the barn for Arrsum. It took quite a bit of money for the material. I have since weathered many different kinds of storms through the years and not all on land. Some were twisters of the soul.

It is said that misfortune runs in pairs, threes and more; well, it could and did. After George's hurricane affair, it happened again. It was a lovely spring day and the men were working in the field getting the ground ready for seeding. My sister Mary's husband came over with his tractor to plow a field for dad. It was something new to us, so when Olga had the lunch made, we all went there to eat with the men in the field and watch the tractor turn the good earth over. Well, we not only watched, but we were invited to ride on the platform of the tractor. The unexpected event did not last long, as there were too many of us for such an area to sit on.

"Maurice fell under the plow," Olga screamed!

Mike couldn't stop quickly enough. One of the wheels ran over Maurice's chest and the plow blade just missed his head. God must have been with him. This really spoiled the day. Not only did Mike get the sound off from dad for allowing so many to ride at one time, but even to consider it when it was so dangerous in the first place!

Dad rushed Maurice home. Mother was there getting ready to go and milk Bluee, as Bluee was milked three times a day. Mother took one look at Maurice and paled, as he looked like a small crushed flower. They took him into the bedroom. He was stripped and checked over for broken bones and anything else. I listened while dad explained to her how it happened. There was an ugly red mark across his chest the width of the wheel which was about five inches wide, no broken bones, or skin. I guess they knew what they were doing. Mother took care of many people—sick, broken bones—and she brought many babies into this world.

After they reassured themselves, mother covered Maurice up and put a cool cloth on his forehead. Mother said a prayer for him and then crossed him and herself.

"Now Frasinia, you stay here and watch him. If he should call for me, you come and get me," mother said.

When mother left, I started to cry because Maurice was whimpering. He looked at me with such hurt and sad eyes. I asked him if it hurt badly. He nodded weakly, as tears spilled over his pale cheeks. I kissed his checks and hands and told him that if he tried to go to sleep, he'd feel better. He closed his eyes, but his breathing was very weak which scared me, so I ran to mama. She was coming into the house with a pail of milk. I told her that Maurice could not breathe very well. She went into his bedroom and checked. He seemed to have fallen asleep. She reassured me that he was sleeping, so I sat down to watch again. Brother Bill relieved me after he had his supper. We all took turns watching Maurice. On the fourth day he started to recover and feel better. With a healthy body and faith in God, he made a good recovery.

Just before school started, Raya and Bill drove the cattle from the summer feeding grounds to home pasture. It seemed Raya was not used to riding in the saddle so she got big saddle sores on her legs. Poor darling, she went through days of pain from infection that set in. Although it may have had nothing to do with Raya's misfortune— other than perhaps that particular day may have been a washday—as I remembered mother wringing clothes out of water that had bluing added to it (Bluing was used to whiten clothes.)—and with mother being busy washing clothes, perhaps that may have been the reason why when Raya would scream with agony, daddy walked the floor with her in his arms. This too passed and Raya's legs healed nicely.

Goodness! I guess it wasn't over yet. Raya got into a grain box and couldn't get out because the ladder was moved from the side of it after she got in without anyone realizing she was in there. The box was resting on the ground. Low and behold a sickle was stored in the box, temporarily, so no one would get hurt. Bill came by when Raya called for help. He reached for her and started to pull her out. In the process of pulling her out, Bill did not know, or see, that she was over the sickle blade. It cut across her knee and down her leg (for which to this day she carries scars). Her leg was bleeding profusely. Mother smothered it with brown puff powder and bandaged it.

(This powder was acquired from a mushroom. It grows like a mushroom except it is like a ball and when it is dried it is full of dry brown powder. This form of mushroom is picked at a certain time of the year and used to stop bleeding. I do believe at the present time it is considered poisonous.)

Mother had tried to teach us the value of wild herbs together at certain times of the year for different uses. Of course she would weed out the ones that were undesirable—the usual weeds.

The Letz family was not quite through with boomerangs. School and snow was blowing in from the four corners of the earth, so it seemed. Horses were lost again—they broke out during the night while seeking shelter from the blinding storm. Dad informed the boys they would have to stay out of school and look for them. Bill, Mike, and Nick dressed up, as warm as it was possible to feel comfortable, to ride the horse and left, but it was still snowing. It had changed to steady snowing and the wind had subsided.

Since the tracks were gone, the boys went different directions hoping that way they would find the animals quicker. That evening Mike and Nick came home late assuming that Bill would all ready be home as they had not seen him in their search for the missing horses.

"Where is Bill?" dad asked.

"We thought he'd be home by now," they said.

"Well, I'll go look for him. Now that it has stopped snowing, there might be tracks to follow; besides he might be with some neighbors," dad said, trying to reassure himself, as the horse galloped out of the yard.

The next morning at breakfast daddy and mother were talking

about his search through the night with no success. Mike and Nick had left earlier that morning to look for Bill and the horses. The sun was so bright that the reflection from the snow was almost blinding. They found Bill and the horses on the way home. It seemed to them as if the horses were coming home by themselves and Bill was just tagging along. They soon discovered that Bill was snow blinded.

"Where did you spend the night, Bill?" they asked him.

"It got dark, so I decided to stay in a cabin that was near by," Bill replied.

What a relief to all when they came into the yard. Bill had to have much tender care, as only mother could give him.

Father added a few more chores to an all ready heavy schedule. The fence had to be checked to make sure that it was in good shape, so there would not be any more of this nightmare. Oh, yes—the cattle and horses had to be brought in for the evening where they could have sheds to bed down in and corrals for the night. Time went by and things returned to normal with everyday living—emotional dilemmas—hurt prides—but no bruises.

Early spring brought ice and mud which spoke louder than words—caution. Mike was trying to steady the horse with soothing words of caution and a gentle guiding hand, but to no avail. The horse slipped and fell on its side hurting Mike's leg and dislocating his shoulder blade. Since his accident happened not far from home and close to the fence, Mike supported himself with the fence on one side and led the horse home.

There always seemed to be someone in the yard during the day, so Mike's difficulty was recognized and they ran out to meet him. He was helped into the house and mother took over the job from there. She checked Mike over for broken bones. Finding none except the dislocated shoulder blade, she set it and put his arm into a sling. His leg had broken skin down the side of the calf which was cleaned and wrapped. Then Mike was told to lie down and rest.

Days seemed to be taken in stride as time went by. I am sure the days of trauma left their mark on the souls of our parents. At least the memories of time gone by still were recalled and remembered, and along with the sad moments there were jolly ones too—like Jim taking his bicycle to go courting, not just across the street, but seven miles on muddy days.

The evening was cool and light frost had crusted the ground and Jim figured that he would be home way before there would be danger of mud like father had warned him.

"Now, Jim, you know that at this time of the year a chinook could start anytime even in the middle of the night. Why don't you take the horse?" dad said.

Jim wanted to show off his new bicycle to the schoolteacher. She was his lady friend in the evenings. He had no problem getting there, but on the way back he had to piggyback the bicycle home. I don't know if he was wiser for his effort; but one thing for sure, he was a very tired young man with mud up to his knees. He had rolled up the pants above his knees, but his shoes suffered inside and out.

Jim took the ribbing graciously and grinned lopsidedly at dad's knowing look, as he recalled dad's warning before he left. Since the morning chores were done, Jim ate breakfast and went to bed for a much needed rest. The teacher learned of his plight, so there was that smile playing about her mouth when she glanced at Jim and he bashfully smiled back.

DROUGHT AND GRASSHOPPERS

Bad follows the good many times through life. It started just too soon in our young lives. Only good thing we had in our favor was people around us who had faced bad times before. Drought and grasshoppers—what could be worse to start out with?

Our neighbor, Pete Peterson, was riding a rig that he had assembled to catch grasshoppers. If, I might say, it was not bad! His wheat field was just across the road from our place. He stopped and came over to get a drink of water from us. Mother was on the backside of the house bending over a washtub doing the washing. Sister Olga was helping mother rinse the clothes, and as for us children, we tried to help hang the clothes, at least the ones we could manage. The men folks were out in the field distributing grasshopper poison.

Now, we had working water and drinking water. When Mr. Peterson asked for a drink of water, mother went to the house to bring him a pitcher of drinking water. Before she returned, Mr. Peterson spied the bucket standing on a bench with a dipper in it. He filled the dipper and drank the water with lice and all. Goodness! Mother was beside herself. She always strained working water too.

"Oh, that's all right Mrs. Letz. What is a little mere meat?" he said and laughed heartily.

We all stared at him with our mouths open and with a sick feeling at the pit of our tummies just thinking how the lice were crawling around inside of him. He looked up at the sky and said,

"Mrs Letz, the war is on. See that big black cloud coming? It's grasshoppers coming to destroy our livelihood."

Mother crossed herself and asked for a measure of courage and help from God. Mr. Peterson thanked mother for the water. Laughing, he waved goodbye to all of us and went back to work. He was a man of great fortitude—not handsome—but likeable and kind. His wife was a lovely and kind person too. They had three children—two girls and a boy. We spent many pleasant times together.

Mrs. Peterson made our first American style dresses. Mother had her order some colored material from Montgomery Ward catalog. It was so sweet how she got around mother in making our dresses.

"Mrs. Letz you are so busy; let me help you out," she said.

Mother was pleased—really—although she was considered quite a seamstress in her own right. Her family was the best and most stylish dressed family back in Europe. The country folk just did not appreciate our unusual styles. Yes—in time we conformed to the American way of life and loved it.

Going back to grasshoppers—they really did a job. It got so bad that cattle suffered from lack of feed and that helped to short change everything else down the line. My brother Jim was working in a flour mill at Glasgow, Montana. As I was too young to comprehend our sudden problem—all knew the grasshoppers were the cause of it and I never ceased to let them forget it. They were so thick that if you had your mouth open you'd be spitting them out. I was on my way to the mailbox to pick up the mail when I was bombarded by them. I was brushing them off my face and arms when I realized I had a couple in my hand. I pulled their wings off and said this is for eating my daddy's crop and mama's garden. Mean little girl, huh?

There was not much of a crop left to harvest, but remember—even the straw was of some nourishment. Daddy and the boys were out in the field harvesting the crop. Mother sent Olga over with lunch for them. It was an outing for all except mama. She may have taken advantage of a few hours to herself.

Raya, Maurice, George and I went with Olga to help carry the lunch, as we thought it would be great to have a picnic with the men. Olga spread the blanket close to the grain wagon to have some shade and placed the food on the blanket. She did not dare leave anything uncovered because of the grasshoppers. The men folk walked up and sat down.

"So you all came to have a picnic with us," daddy said. "Just be careful the grasshoppers don't beat you to it."

He was right. They were landing in the plates and barely missing our mouths.

"Olga, I swallowed a grasshopper. He is scratching my throat," George screamed.

Daddy tried to have him cough it out by patting him on his back.

"Well, son, I guess it will have to be part of your lunch. It won't hurt you."

Dad held him a while in his arms until George composed himself and started eating his lunch again. The men went back to work and we gathered the pans and blanket and started walking across the field for home.

Next thing I knew we were moving to Glasgow, Montana, to live until better times. Since the move was late in the summer, there was danger of snow following at the heels of the cattle drive to Glasgow. Dad sent mother and most of us young children by train. He loaded pigs, chickens and everything else that couldn't follow the herd and horses in the wagons.

In the meantime, Jim had leased a farm in Havre, Montana, for us to live on, but since there was no school close by, we were to live with Jim in Glasgow until school was out. That is the way it had to be. He was our sole supporter in time of need.

Let me assure you—we found that we just could not love all the teachers, but fear this one, we did! She used to take pleasure in asking a child to bring her a short piece of rubber hose to spank a child in front of the whole class. She would suspend the child between two chairs and strike him or her.

There seemed to be one little boy (Chester) that got the hose more than others. It just did not seem right. His mother came to school and wanted to know why? After all, her little boy was only six years old. He couldn't possibly be that bad, and really he was not. She was a mean teacher. I remained in the room just to tell his mother what went on, but I was sent out of the room, maybe for the best. Chester was taken out of this school to go to another one. I learned this from some of the children that knew his parents. Something must have happened, or taken place, because there was no hose used after that, but the sharp edged ruler was still carried around in her hand.

We were very happy when school was out and we got to go to the farm. It was our first experience with city life and we agreed that the city folk could have it. What a reunion we had when we got to the farm. Daddy was happy to have all of us home. Of course, the calves, lambs, chickens and a few other things were surprised to be invaded by a mob of frisky creatures. They had forgotten us in nine months time.

DEAD EYE MAURICE

You have heard of "Dead Eye Dick," for his quick and accurate shooting? Well—my little brother Maurice was such—even at his tender age of five years old. He learned to shoot the .22 rifle from his older brothers' instruction and surpassed them. It seemed as if the last of us four children spent lots of time together. We'd go gopher and rabbit hunting and did a good job of shooting, but Maurice would hit the spot where he'd say he would.

Mother was out in the yard trying to catch some chicken for dinner. Maurice came up with his gun to help.

"Maurice, put that gun away before you get hurt, or hurt someone else," mother called out.

"Mother, I'll shoot any chicken you want right through the eye."

He did just that—all five of them. Mother was aghast at such accurate shooting. One day after lunch Maurice went horseback riding, bareback like a little Indian. A few hours later he rode up by the kitchen door.

"Hey! Frasinia, look what I got—a snake," he said.

I looked out through the kitchen door and sure enough he had a snake lassoed by the neck dragging along behind the horse, and I said,

"Weren't you afraid of it?"

"It's dead. I shot him right through the eye from the horse." he said.

His laughter rang with pride. He looked like a beautiful butterfly ready to take to the wing. He was a small child for his age. He was an excellent rider and shooter. He'd hold the reins and the horse's mane together and race with the wind.

Thinking about it now, he had a right to be proud. We were proud of him too, but we were also very concerned for his life. He was the most even tempered child and most forgiving in the family, and yet to this day, I do believe he carries the title of being the best shot, at least in our family.

MY FIRST TRIP ALONE

Just before school started, the folks received a letter from my sister Mary, asking to please send Olga to help out with babysitting. Olga was the oldest, and mother needed her at home to help with the work. I was selected to go in her place. I was nine years old, and this was my first trip alone anywhere without my family. The preparation for my trip was done in a quiet manner. If there was any feeling of sadness, it was not expressed—I suppose for my sake. After all, I was going to see my sister who loved me.

The day arrived when I was to leave and our good neighbor Steve came over with horse and wagon to take me along to town where I was to catch the train. He had to go in for some shopping, so he was kind enough to take me and see that I was safely put on the train. Mother handed me my lunch which was put in a paper sack and tied up in a dish towel, so it could be carried easily; and another one just like it held my clothes. She kissed me goodbye and said, as she held me close,

"Now be a good girl and mind your sister."

"Frasinia, if you want to come home just let us know and we will send for you," father said.

He hugged and kissed me. Bill was the only one who had tears in his eyes and he said,

"I'll miss you."

The rest said they wished they were going with me. Best offer I had that day. It gave the folks a vacation with one less to out think, during the waking hours, I am sure.

When we arrived in Havre, Montana, it was about an hour before train time. Steve took me to lunch. It was my first time having lunch out in public, at least that I remembered. Then we went to the train and into the coach. Steve sat me down and said,

"Frasinia, stay here—I'll be right back."

He was back in a short time and brought me a gift—a beautiful blue ribbon with red roses on it. I was all eyes, as I never had such a pretty ribbon that I could recall. (Now, Steve didn't know, but here was a little girl in love with a twenty-seven year old man.)

Going down to Havre, he sang songs and told me stories in Russian which helped to pass the time away as it took six hours to get there. He tied the ribbon on my braid and kissed me goodbye on my cheek. He stood on the platform smiling and waving to me. I waved back at him until I could not see him anymore.

The trains were not air-conditioned at that time, so before long my food started sending out aromas which started to nauseate me. Actually, I was getting train sick, but I did not know and thought it was the food. I opened up the window and pushed all the food out between the bars of the window—(whole roasted chicken, loaf of bread, and four apples). There were two men alongside the train track smiling up at me. I heard a voice beside me and I looked up and saw a lady standing beside my seat.

"Honey, don't throw your food away; you'll need it," she said.

"I can't eat it; it smells and is making me sick," I said.

By this time the conductor stopped and said,

"Little girl, do you have any money?"

I showed him my coins which added up to twenty cents. He shook his head and walked away.

I woke up the next morning and found that I was covered with a man's coat. I looked up and there was the same lady leaning over me and she said,

"That is my husband's coat. You seemed chilly and restless last night."

I looked down quickly as I missed the feeling of my drawstring coin bag on my wrist. The woman's eyes followed my dismayed look.

"What is it, dear?"

"My coin bag is gone!" I said.

I looked under the seat and further, but to no avail.

"It really is gone!" I continued.

Not in the habit of having money I did not let it bother me for long. I think it was the little silk bag I missed most.

"Come on honey, let's go and get cleaned up," the lady said.

She had two little girls of her own, and she took them along to the bathroom. She washed us and combed our hair. She taught me how to use the indoor water closet. We went back to our seats, and I no sooner got settled when the conductor came to me and said,

"Follow me little girl."

As we were trained to obey the elders and had no fear of people, I stood up and followed him. I was led to the dining room. He pulled the chair out and told me to sit down. I did. The colored man brought me a bowl of oatmeal, milk, toast and orange juice. He smiled at me, as I proceeded to tell him that I could not pay for the breakfast. He pointed to an elderly man and said,

"He will pay for it, little girl."

My—that was a tasty breakfast, and I was hungry. I was taken care of by some kind person all through my trip. It took three nights and three days to reach my destination. Lucky me—that man was going my way.

Mary was so happy to see me, and she listened to me relating my train trip, which to me had been exciting. I told her about the water closet and how it worked. She laughed with delight at my experience. She led me into the house to meet her new baby boy Malvin who was eleven months old. My—he was a big baby boy and I wondered if I would be able to lift him, as I was a frail little girl. I recalled the conversation a while back that I had heard between my parents thinking that I was asleep.

"I don't know what to do with that child; she just won't eat," mother said.

"Oh—don't worry too much, mother; she'll eat when she gets hungry," dad answered.

"But she is so finicky about her food too," mother continued.

"Yes, but don't let her know about it; otherwise, we will have a problem," dad countered.

"I just wish she would eat like Raya. She gives us no problem," mother said.

Boy, this bit of concern, that I did not know, really opened up a new field for me, but not for long. Dad's predication came true and to this day, I enjoy food.

Sister had two little girls—Raya and Stella. It did not take us long to get acquainted and we spent many pleasant days together, while Mary would attend to her large garden and many household duties.

When school started, I was taken there the first day by my sister. She had to take her children along. She carried Malvin and I walked with Stella and Raya hand-in-hand. It was a mile away through the woods on a beaten path. It was lovely. Blackberry and raspberry bushes were growing along the way. Mary wouldn't let me eat any as she said I'd get stained and soiled for school.

"Perhaps on the way home you can eat some," she said.

School was fun to me; I got acquainted with the children who went my way. We would stop to pick berries after school and hop and skip all the way home. Finally—I was accepted into a group of young children called the "Fruit Pickers Club."

Early one Saturday morning, we met at the gate of someone's beautiful orchard. I had a five pound lard bucket with me thinking it was like our berry picking times back home. I noticed there was a lovely home in the background. We all walked through the gate and quickly climbed the trees. I happened to get a tree with long sharp needles about three inches long growing upright. It was a prune tree. After eating a few, I managed to get out of it with a few scratches and a ripped dress. My next tree was a luscious plum tree. It seemed that most of us children were in it.

When I heard someone say, "The caretaker—run." the boys and girls seemed to drop out of the tree and run in every direction and, as for me—well, I had my eyes on a juicy purple plum on the very tip of the branch and I was determined to get it.

"Little girl, you better get down, or you'll fall," the voice said to me.

Looking up at the man, I said, "Oh, I just want to get this plum."

And I did. I got down and showed him the fruit I had picked and asked if he'd like some.

"Don't you know you are not supposed to pick fruit off the trees here?" he asked.

I looked at him—still without any fear and said,

"I didn't know."

Looking around to see if there were any of the other children about, he noticed that I was looking for other children and said,

"They know they are not to do this—that is why they ran away.

He told me he was the caretaker while the people were away on their vacation. Then I noticed he had a gun. So—I offered the fruit back to him. He told me to keep it, but never to come there again or to go picking fruit in anybody else's yard again without permission from the owners. I walked gingerly through the gate and home to my sister. She asked me where I got the fruit. I told her what happened.

"You were lucky he didn't shoot you!"

Mary then proceeded to clue me on what the children were doing and not to listen to them again. Next morning the children surrounded me with questions—how I got away and did they take the fruit away from me. I told them that I got to keep the fruit and just walked through the gate. They all looked at me with wonder. I suppose, if I was worldlier, I could have been their leader, but just then I spied my little girlfriend—bless her heart. She was more important at the time to me. She told me she had the same experience with them. This gave us a reason for a stronger friendship.

School days went by fast and spring came with all its glory. I was enjoying myself, as I had made a few more nice friends. I can't say that I was homesick for any long period at a time—just too many things to do. I forgot to mention that Mary lived in Bellingham, Washington. The ocean was only a hop and skip from her home; it was beautiful there. It was a resort area.

The folks must have missed me more, as they sent my brother Jim over to see what was going on. I was sent home and Jim stayed on for some time. I learned later in life that Mary's husband was abusive to her and that was why the folks never refused her our company. It helped to keep him in line. He was afraid of her brothers. I must have been the informer as to his behavior toward Mary.

I arrived at Brady, Montana, as my folks had moved back there since I left home. Thinking that daddy was going to meet me, instead I was met by some friends of the folks. They told me that I was to stay with them for a few days, as my folks would not be able to come for me until then.

The next morning was Sunday, so after breakfast I went outside to play. The lady asked me if I would like to attend church with them.

"No! I'll just stay here and play," I said.

While they were gone I decided to go home, without giving a second thought to what problem I'd create for the nice people. I set out in the direction where I recalled my home was. I ran, hopped, skipped, and walked along the dirt road. After some time a car pulled alongside me. It happened to be a farm family that we knew.

"Why Rose, (My name is Frasinia Rose and lots of people called me Rose) what are you doing way out here by yourself?" he asked.

"I am going home." I answered.

"Do your folks know you are coming?" he asked.

He told me to get in the car. While driving to his home I explained to him what was told to me.

"Rose, do you know what you have done to those nice people?" he asked.

I shook my head, "no." Then he proceeded to explain to me how inconsiderate I was. My—that made me feel very bad and I started to cry. I told him I'd go back to those people and wait for my folks.

"I'll see if I can reach them by phone and explain," he said.

Soon as we reached their place, he called. They were up in arms about me, as one was home by the phone and the other was out looking for me. I was crying and his wife put her arms around me and said not to cry anymore—but just to never do it again. I said I just wanted to see my folks, as I had not seen them for so long.

It was noon so we had dinner and shortly after that they drove me home. These folks lived halfway between Brady and our place. It was fifteen miles from Brady to our place, so it seems I had walked almost six miles before they picked me up.

The folks were surprised to see me but happy to know that I was safe. Of course more scolding was dished out to me. They thanked the Banks for being so kind and easing the worry for the folks in town. Daddy had to go into town for my clothes a week later.

Goodness! I thought I had grown up considerably—not in size, but in ways of the world, so I thought. I must explain to you why we had no fear of distance, or danger. It was nothing for mother to send us children on errands, or with messages. It could be a mile, or seven miles. Father used to lease land six miles from our homestead. I recall going with Maurice to take a message to daddy. We started out early in the morning—barefooted as it was a warm summer day.

Daddy was angry with mother for taking such a chance with so many snakes about at that time and so few people traveling. In fact, we didn't meet one soul in that distance. He finished his day's work and left for home with horse and wagon. He asked us children what we did when we saw a snake.

"Oh, we just stop until it goes by and then we go," we answered.

And we did just that, that very day. It was quite a ways ahead of us crossing the road. He said that was a wise thing to do and patted us on the head.

Daddy asked mama how she dared take such chances with us

little children, after all it was not like in Russia where there would be some other soul walking every few minutes, or hour. He told her that we saw a big snake that day. She told him how she warned us to leave snakes and wild animals alone. Dad responded with concern and said,

"Good heaven! What if the animals don't leave them alone?"

"You have to trust in God," she said.

STRIPPING FEATHERS

Stripping feathers was considered a pastime in our family, but a very necessary job to be done. It was no effort on our parents' part to entice us as they made a delightful game of it. It was usually done during the cold winter evenings. Mother made sure that seeds from pumpkins, cucumbers, sunflowers, muskmelons, and other seed factors, that were edible, were roasted and ready to take the place of nuts. Now these were mixed together in a big flour sack.

You'd be surprised that many times the seeds almost did fill the sack. This we enjoyed and looked forward to—with story telling. Of course we knew we couldn't strip feathers and spit out the seed shells. But storytelling went with feather stripping and treats came after. Sometimes it came as a surprise to us—I mean stripping feathers; after all, one can forget about such things through the spring and summer months. We'd try to sneak out if we became aware of such a setting, but where can one hide with such a bloodhound family. Mother was always busy picking up loose feathers in different corners of the yard and chicken house.

Then there was the stripping of the geese before they started to lose their precious downy robes. When she got through with them they looked like they were ready for singeing and the cooking pot. When mother released them, they made such noise and flapped their wings, at least what was left of them, and staggered away, but mother never lost a goose—it was cooked first.

I'll never forget my first experience with this delightful pastime, as it was called. Mother had a couple galvanized tubs in the living room and a sack of feathers; then she or dad would show us how to strip the feathers. Speaking cheerfully, making it seem like such fun, mother usually would say,

"Now, this will be your pillow, or feather mattress—isn't that nice."

Dad told stories which left us starry eyed and hungry for more. The fine down would tickle our noses and get into our hair, clothes and cling on our eyelashes, but that was nothing! The older brothers and sisters joined in this big project too, as they had no choice. Time went by and before we knew it, pillows and other sleeping apparel were made to keep everybody comfy through the winter months. When a daughter married she usually got four pillows, downy quilt, and a feather mattress as part of her dowry. Many colds months were spent making dowries. Dear mother was tenderhearted, even with the boys' brides. We thought she was overdoing it, but our opinion was overruled.

CHURNING BUTTER

Churning butter was done twice a week by Raya and me. Today was Raya's turn and I had to clean the house. Well—it just seemed not to be Raya's day. She was impatient to go out horseback riding and mother had other ideas. We had a five gallon blue porcelain churn that was suspended on a four-legged frame. Mother had it all ready to go and called Raya to get busy. She noticed Raya was not in her cheerful mood.

"Raya, you just calm down, and soon as you get through here, you can go riding." mother said.

"But mother," she said, "Maurice and George will be gone and I wanted to go with them. They are going to hunt rabbits and gophers."

It seemed that Maurice and George had to get the cattle out of one pasture field and put them into another, and they were going to mix pleasure with business. It would have been fun as we four used to do this quite often.

"You'll just have to do it some other time then, or if you get through sooner you can go and meet them," mother said.

From hurrying, the churn spun off the stand and the lid flew open. Raya rushed to right the churn to save some of the cream; and she not only calmed down, but she was stultified at extra work and besides what mother would say of wasted cream. Just then in walked Mike. He tried not to laugh because he noticed our frantic effort of picking up the cream. The more we tried; the more it smeared. The cloth was oozing with rich-cream. Besides, I was trying to get Raya to help wipe it up and she rebelled; all she wanted to do was cry. I did not blame her, but I needed help, so I threw a rag at her and told her to get busy and she threw it back at me. Well, it just turned out to be a tug of war.

"Raya, you have to help, so we can get it cleaned up before mother comes in."

"I don't care; I won't do it," she said.

"But you did it because you spun it too fast," I said.

"Girls, girls, stop it," Mike said. "I have an idea."

He opened the door and in walked the three little pigs. Now these were not the three little pigs from the fairy tales, but they did the job. They were the orphans that were bottle fed and thought they were human. They would follow us about the yard and were "Johnny on the spot" to get warm milk from the cows when it was milking time. They did not know what it was to eat with their kind and cared less. They would eat with the animals and in the yard. If we were in the yard talking they would make pig noises and look from one to the other. With all the slipping and sliding they did, they really were a big help. Finally the floor was clean enough to be scrubbed with hot suds. Mike shooed the staggering cream smeared pigs out of the house.

"All we have to worry about is that they don't get sick," Mike said laughing.

Mike cleaned the spots on the ceiling and other high spots. We all really worked fast to get finished. We were all fast workers and quite efficient. I even filled the churn with more cream and had a much calmer Raya back to churning butter. When mother came in she wondered why the butter wasn't churned yet, and as we did not give any comments, she went about her duties. That week we had less butter to sell. One just can't win all the time when tempers fly, or was it the butter churn?

HOLD ON RAYA

After we milked the cows and separated the milk, we put the fresh cream into milk cans to take to the creamery in the small town of Conrad, Montana, just three miles from the farm. This was done at least twice a week. With two 5-gallon cans of cream and a couple cases of eggs, we were ready to leave for the city. Bill hitched Pacer up to a light weight one horse buggy and said,

"Frasinia, just hold the reins firm, but not too tight and you'll have no trouble. He is a much safer horse than old spooky Star."

Since I had ridden Pacer at different times, I had no thought of fear from him. My niece Raya went along with me for the ride. Raya was my sister's little girl; they were staying with us at the time. We were both sitting on the seat at peace with the world. Pacer was behaving beautifully until a car horn was tooted, as they went by.

"Raya, hold on to me," I screamed.

She didn't utter a word but wrapped her little arms around my waist and held on for dear life. I braced my feet against the front panel and held on with both hands to the reins.

Pacer didn't stop running until we drove to the edge of the town and a couple of men ran out from the livery stable and caught hold of the bridle and stopped him. He was all lathered with white foam and shaking like a leaf. It seems that the folks in the car, that caused the runaway, had told the livery men of the runaway horse and to help us. The livery stable was on the outskirts of the town.

Raya and I were frightened out of our wits, but we recovered after a short period. Guess we had too many of such wild rides before. The men took the eggs and the cream to the creamery. With the wild ride that we had, the eggs and the cream were all intact, thank goodness!

The man took Pacer into the livery stable and unhitched him from the buggy; then he proceeded to give Pacer a royal treatment. He spoke to him gently while rubbing him down. He gave him a drink and some oats. Raya and I went down town to do some shopping for mother, after the man convinced me that all would be fine and ready when we returned from shopping.

It did not take long to do the shopping and we were back in a short time. While we were gone, the men had decided that one of them had to take us back home to make sure we'd be safe. One explained to me that they hitched another horse to the buggy because Pacer was still too nervous and he was just tied to the buggy.

On the way back the man told me that it was a wonder Raya and I and the horse were alive. Pacer should never be used for such jobs he was not trained for, as he was a thoroughbred, he informed me. Of course I didn't know, or understand the dignity of horses, or men. All I knew was we had jobs to do and no questions were asked. He told me that he knew my father and brothers and he wanted to talk to them.

We arrived home at noon and the men folk were home having their dinner. Dad asked the man to have dinner, which he accepted with pleasure, as he had not eaten yet. He explained what took place and what a tragedy it could have been. The folks were very grateful for the heroic effort. Dad explained that perhaps mother and he assumed too much of a 14-year old girl, but I seemed to be able to handle Pacer so well when I rode him.

"It is a greater danger, Mr. Letz," he said, "if the horse is a racehorse."

After that hair-raising experience, the family was more cautious which noble beast did what job. As for us there was no discrimination and no job too lowly.

SLOPPING PIGS

During spring and summer, when so much field work was done, the men left to work with the dawn and returned home with the setting sun. This left the home work to the women folk and younger children. Since mother was the only woman and the rest her loving brood, jobs were assigned to each one.

After early breakfast, Raya and I went to milk cows. We usually had 25 to 30 head of cows to milk. It so happened that this particular spring there was only 25. We considered ourselves top-speed milkers—from five to ten minutes per cow, as it left an uneven number for the two of us. Milking twice a day took care of that. Mother didn't have any special cow, that needed her personal touch anymore, as Bluee had departed many moons before from our family. Soon as the cows were milked, we had to separate the milk.

The fresh separated cream was stored in the cellar to keep cool as well as extra milk for day use. We had two root cellars—one was a ways from the house and used for smoking meat and whatever else needed smoking. The other was a cellar under the house with an extra door to enter in besides a trapdoor in the house. The cellar under the house was not finished off with concrete, as mother used part of it for a winter garden and in one corner to store goods from the garden, or fresh fruit that kept for some time.

Feeding pigs were next on the list. Raya and I took the separated milk and mixed barley into it and with whatever was gathered from preparing meals and other goodies that were not eaten up by the family was given to the noble snouts.

Now—this rooting family of fifty was fenced in on the backside of the reservoir dam which gave them a natural stream to root in below the dam where the water seeped through, and in places they even made themselves—a tub to wallow in. The pigs had to walk up a slight incline to their eating place. This consisted of two troughs, each twenty-five feet long. Well, I never saw such a mess.

They were the most impatient and inconsiderate hog family ever to grace their table. We did not have a chance to finish filling their troughs before their snouts were pushing helter-skelter. I happened to find myself pushed back and fourth in the trough. How it happened was a great surprise to me. I was just trying to empty the bucket out and the big pig stuck his snout into it and flipped me into the gooey trough. Slippery as it was and with the help of the other pigs, I was pushed back and forth. Every time I tried to get out—well—I was pushed about like a yo-yo.

I heard peals of laughter which turned out to be my darling sister Raya. It must have been a sight! Finally a big pig threw me out with his snout. That must have been his good deed of the day. I rose up off the ground. We finished putting in the rest of the feed. Then we walked to the reservoir and I walked into the water to clean off my clothes and all.

When we came into the house, mother was mixing bread. She was surprised at my appearance. I went to change into dry clothes. I could hear Raya telling mother what happened. It turned out to be a hilarious day for all, including me.

We all had our share of pulling weeds in the garden and yard. When the weeds were pulled, they were hauled in the little red wagon to the pigs. They seemed to relish the delightful spring salad. With different types of weeds, it had its own spice seasoning.

Maurice and George had to clean the cow and horse barns and fill the mangers with feed. Bill had graduated to fieldwork with the rest of the men. Mother took care of the poultry and other many household duties. Of course we had to help mother in the house when we were through with outside work.

Many times while slopping the pigs, we took time to lie down on the beautiful green grass on the hilltop and gaze at the sky. It was one of our inspiring moments—even poetry fell from our lips. Such a delightful day to dream—only to be awakened by the call of mother's sweet voice,

"What's taking you girls so long?"

"Coming, mother," we'd call to her.

BIRDS OF A FEATHER

The birds of a feather flock together,
making a sight so grand;
I know they are heading for the sunny land,
they held a meeting which was fleeting.
As they prattled, it was settled,
while the cold breeze blew the autumn leaves by;
the birds rose, as one, into the big blue sky.
By Frasinia Rose Letz—1925

DAD'S UNFORGETTABLE CAR RIDE

Dad was coming home—what joy to us all—as he had been gone a whole week. The train was due at 5:30 p.m. (We lived three miles or so from Conrad, Montana, on a farm.) My darling brother Maurice (10 years old) took it upon himself to go get dad. What other better chance did he have to drive the car than when all the men were out in the field? I am sure this was going through his mind, as we never saw him at a loss of what to do.

George was usually around him, but today he kept busy carving animals out of wood that he had sketched out. He was the artistic fellow and blessed to be gifted with the talent.

Now—really, dad's intentions were to walk home, as that was no great distance at all to walk, and besides if he was lucky, someone might pick him up. Maurice ran and opened the yard gate and then proceeded to open the garage door. He got into the car and started it up. Mother, hearing the motor running, ran to the garage and tried to stop him by talking him out of it, but to no avail, so in her excitement she closed the door.

"Mother if you don't open the door, I'll back right through it," Maurice called out.

What could poor mother do, but open the door and step aside. She did scream at him, that he'd hurt himself and perhaps others, but he smiled at her and drove out of the yard onto the highway—scattering the chickens on both sides of the car. Such noise, you never heard! One chicken wasn't so lucky; it got a broken leg. How many ended up with heart trouble was hard to tell, as many never lived too long to find that out.

Maurice got safely to town. How did we know? Well, he came home in one piece. It seemed he had stopped in the nick of time to keep from going through the creamery window. The creamery was right next to the depot. Dad was there all ready and saw all the commotion, before he realized who was driving the car. Everybody seemed to be stepping lively to keep out of the way.

Maurice was small for his age, so he was looking through the steering wheel to see where he was driving. At first glance, one would assume it was a runaway car. This caused quite a gathering—just what Maurice needed and poor dad was stymied as to how to answer questions that were thrown at him. It was doubly hard for him not being able to carry on a conversation in English very well at the time.

"How come you allow a child to drive at such a tender age?"

"Dad knew I was coming, and besides I know how to drive," Maurice answered confidently.

After the first shock wore off, a nice and understanding gentleman backed the car off the wooden walk and headed it towards home. Dad was reluctant to get into the car, but he decided he should for Maurice's sake. Besides the little iron man with all the confidence was sitting behind the wheel promising a safe trip home. When they got home dad was somewhat pale, but smiling.

"I don't know how we got home in one piece. That boy can't even see over the wheel," dad told mother.

Mother told dad of the problem she had in trying to keep Maurice from taking the car. Now, this car belonged to our older brothers, Mike and Nick. Maurice would have to answer to them for using it without their permission. Much to everybody's surprise, they were amazed at his knowledge to drive without instruction. Little did they know how observant of their driving he had been while going for rides with them. He always ended up riding in the front. There was a reason for his rides. From then on, his driving of the car was forbidden until he was of age. Even to this day he doesn't have much trouble in doing things that he puts his mind to do.

Dad had many runaway horses to contend with, but somehow he was always able to tame and control them. Now this iron machine was something else he had not taken the trouble to conquer. Perhaps there would not have been quite as much to fear if he knew how to drive it. It was something else too—to have it driven by a child who had no fear of it.

L to R: Frasinia Rose Dolack, George Montgomery, Raya Lyda Markson (1991), and oil painting of their parents Gregory and Duna (Dena) Letz

L to R: Raya Lyda Markson, Frasinia Rose Dolack and Dolls

L to R: Tony and Donna Dolack, Beth and Gary Dolack, Frank and Frasinia Rose Dolack

Frasinia Rose Dolack and one of her oil paintings, 2004

L to R: Nancy Guild, George Montgomery, Milton, Frasinia Rose, Marlene and Arthur on the set of 20th Century-Fox film The Brasher Doubloon, starring George Montgomery and Nancy Guild

L to R: Landgren family: Marlene, Arthur, Milton, Frasinia Rose, 1946

Olga and Mike at Brady, Montana

Willey family: John "Bud," Marlene, Dan Brenda and Debra

Center: Jan and Milton Landgren, 1977

FISHING IN IRRIGATION DITCH

In the year of 1922, we moved to Conrad, Montana, an irrigation farm. It seemed we moved quite often in the years between 1919 through 1927. The great drought and grasshoppers seemed to follow shortly after the First World War. Strange—the countryside seemed to suffer in sympathy with the war torn countries across the great waters. It really got sick, so sick that it could not provide food for its people, so the people moved about hoping that somewhere the country was recovering from the pain enough to give them food. So much was dependent on mother earth! As our homestead was dryland farming, mother and dad decided to make a move to irrigation farming. Dad leased this place in the fall of 1922. Most of the cattle and horses were moved there right after summer work was done and whatever else there was to gather from the sick earth.

Mike and Bill were batching at the rental place all ready. As I was the oldest of the girls now at home, mother decided that I should go there and clean up the house, before she and the rest of the family came. Dad would help me with heavy things and then there were two brothers to help. I was delighted to go.

Early before daybreak we started out from our homestead, fifteen miles east of Brady, Montana. Dad had loaded chickens in big box crates and other species of poultry. The furniture, mattresses, and bedding were placed on top of the crates in the wagon that was pulled by a couple of draft horses and I was the official driver. Dad had another such rig ready with pigs and feed for them and the chickens. Our food was coming along for us too. Of course with such a big move many trips had been made all ready.

"Frasinia, just hold the reins firm, but not too tight and they'll go along nicely, as they will follow my load," dad said.

Smart horses—they did just that and left me to dream a bit and look around the countryside. The daylight was coming to an end and the night was quietly slipping in. Before long it was dark. I could hardly make out the objects around me. I must say the horses still had their senses about them—good for all of us! I heard a horse galloping and next thing I knew someone was beside me. I tried drawing away— ready to call out for dad.

"Oh, sis, it's me, Mike," as he took the reins from my hands. "Calm down now. I just think you need help."

"I sure do, but how did you come so quietly?" I asked.

"You were probably dreaming and did not hear me," he said.

"Yes, I was so engrossed in listening to the night noises and as to where we were traveling that I missed the noise you made getting on the wagon box."

"Well, we are not too far from there now," he said; "dad just entered the yard."

"Notice the fence? You know you have to look down too, not just around in the dark," Mike continued.

"No wonder I couldn't see much. I was looking around in the dark instead of down from my perch," I laughed.

"Frasinia, are you all right?" dad called out.

"Just fine! Mike is with me," I said.

"Good, but how did I miss hearing you son?" dad asked.

"Oh, I was coming home from town and you were all ready ahead of me," Mike answered.

We got there without any mishap. Bill was happy to see us and had a stew ready. I must say it tasted good. He had shot a rabbit that morning and surprised us with his hand at cooking. When I woke up the next morning, dad had a boiler filled with water sitting on the back of the stove; the water was steaming hot. Dad had breakfast ready too, bless him.

"Daughter, eat now and then we will get busy with house cleaning," dad said.

For the next few days we worked. Dad helped too, and the boys carried water in and out when they were not taking care of the chores. Dad was anxious to get us all together before snow started flying, and besides school was going to start in a week. That weekend dad and Mike left early for home to pick up the last of the remains and mother, Maurice, George and Raya. It was nice to be together again.

School and new friends and teacher—by this time we were very much Americanized in clothes and manners. Our teacher taught classes from first through eighth grade. There were 32 children and all in one room. At one end of the room, a big potbelly heater stood ready to do its bit of work in keeping us warm—providing it was fed heartily. In the hall entrance along one side of the wall we hung up our wraps and on the other side a long bench held a water bucket with a cover on it; the bucket had a spigot. There were four wash basins and a few towels hanging on nails to be used for drying our grimy little hands. We had to bring our own drinking cups from home and keep them in our desk. The families took turns washing the towels.

What a year! School days went by so fast. We had the most enjoyable teacher to be around. We learned about school Roundup and what it was all about. It was fun preparing for it. She made it so exciting that we went all out, and we even surprised ourselves at what we could do.

The big Roundup came; it was held in Conrad, Montana. Conrad was a small farmers' town, and it depended on their business. For our first experience of the Roundup, Miss Russell our teacher went with her pupils to see the exhibits from different schools. (We were like chicks with a mother hen.) Of course we had to compete with other schools in different fetes and competition. I still can remember my teacher saying,

"Frasinia, now it is your turn to throw the basketball."

I was so interested in others that I forgot my turn. I must have done well, as I saw a big smile on Miss Russell's face. The last day of the Roundup we took in the show—Bill, Raya, Maurice, George and me. While Bill was getting our tickets, I noticed Miss Russell was standing in line to see the show too. Since Bill was two years older than I, he paid full price. I was so young looking that I could have passed for 10 years old, and I could very easily have gotten in for the half-ticket fare, but oh no, not me. I wanted everybody to know I was twelve years old.

"Frasinia, you are not twelve yet," Miss Russell said, with a smile.

"Oh, but I am, don't you know?" I said proudly.

She blushed and said, "Oh!"

After the show we drove home chattering like magpies about the picture we saw. The Roundup lasted three days. I stayed with the sheriff's daughter that my family knew and the rest stayed in a hotel where the teacher and the other children stayed.

Sunday morning found us telling our folks of our experience in the city and all about Roundup. Mother and dad enjoyed hearing all about it, as much as we enjoyed it and telling them about it.

Monday morning was another happy event for our teacher, as well as for the children. I got a first place blue ribbon in basketball throw and running and for my embroidery work and Bill for leather work. It seemed the whole class came back with all kinds of prizes.

My brother Jim came home a few days before school was out. Many times he would drive us over to the school if the weather was stormy, or colder than usual. He was on his vacation. He had been working in the flour mill in Glasgow, Montana, but dad asked him to come home and go on crop sharing with him. Jim was still single. Jim always took us early to school to help the teacher with starting the heater. She was uneasy while he was there because we children behaved as if there were a big romance in progress. Jim would bring enough fuel to last all day. We even tried to help by asking her over to dinner.

She did come over and Jim was a perfect gentleman. He even took her to a show while he was home, but three weeks was just too short. As he was leaving to go back to work, he told dad that he really didn't have enough land to share, as he was planning to get married to a girl in Glasgow. It seemed that he had been going with her for quite a while. They were a family of Catholics, and they wanted him to change to their religion before the parents would consent to a marriage. He asked mother and dad how they felt about it.

"I came home to think about it and ask you folks to help me decide what is right, Jim said.

"Son, how can we help you? Do you feel that your love is big and deep enough for her to give up your belief and be happy with her? If so, then let your heart be your guide," dad said.

Jim sighed with tears in his eyes and hugged dad and mother, placing a kiss on their checks.

"Guess I'll be leaving tomorrow morning, so I better get my things together," he said.

Miss Russell missed Jim bringing us over so she asked where he was. We told her he went to Glasgow to work and to see his girlfriend. She smiled and never asked about him again. He wrote home in Russian often and informed the folks of his studying to become a Catholic. Our large family was getting smaller even before we moved to the irrigation farm. Jim worked and lived at Glasgow, Montana; Nick lived with a family in Standwood, Washington, going to a barber school. Sister Olga was in Matlin Falls, Washington, helping Mary with housework and children as Mary had had an operation. Only six busy bodies were still at home with the folks.

Spring was greeted with a walk in the crisp morning. Five of us decided to get acquainted with the countryside. The sun was warming the day rather slowly. We took our shoes off to walk across the paper thin ice that crackled under our feet in small puddles of water. It led us to a big irrigation flume high above the ground. This didn't present any problem to us at all! We climbed up the crisscross pillars that held up the flume and slid down the side of an empty flume and walked to the end where it rested on level ground. Feeling the pangs of hunger, we started for home.

My! We hardly realized how far we traveled which proved to be quite a ways. We were looking forward to a warm meal. Mother usually had a large pot of Borscht, or some delicious stew, cooking slowly on the back of the cooking range. We saw plenty of countryside and a few neighbors sparingly settled in that community. I guess we surprised them too by greeting spring with bare feet. The day ended with exciting thoughts for a better year.

The crops were seeded and a garden planted with prayers for a good return. It was a good year. Water helped a lot, but even the dryland farming had better luck. Dad decided to lease another place, as he was a dryland farmer at heart. Of course he probably had Jim in his mind yet. Dad realized the importance of getting back on his feet, and the water played in supplying much needed moisture to quench mother earth's thirst.

During irrigation time, the fish were bountiful in the ditches, especially where the head gates were. I was in the garden pulling weeds when I heard the water rushing in. I ran over to take a look. What a sight! I walked in and started to grab the fish with bare hands—beautiful fish of all sizes churning around me. I managed to catch a few and throw them out, and then I picked up a bucket that was handy in the garden and tried catching them that way, which was better.

In the process of my fishing, I was soaked to the skin. What a sight I must have presented to mother. I went to the house with a bucket full of different size fish—mother's favorite food. I was simply beside myself with joy.

"Frasinia, where did you get the fish? Did someone give them to you?" mother asked.

Before I got through explaining, there were other ears listening and what an exciting moment—to be sure! Maurice, George, Raya and I ran out there to get more fish with more buckets. When we got back to the fish, the fish had spread down into the ditch from the head gate, so the fishing game settled into regular every day pleasure, as long as there was water in the ditches. This was our first experience with irrigation on a farm. It was not only our fishing spot, but swimming hole, as well.

Our swimming apparel was something else. Usually we wore the same clothes we had on for swimming. We'd let the sun dry the clothes right on us. My! Our days were filled with many simple, but joyous, hours after our assigned duties were fulfilled. Healthy morale builder—as dad and mother would say.

Summer passed with a bountiful harvest for the first time in three years. The garden was a joy to look at and eat from. Wheat and oats were great; in fact Thanksgiving Day rang loudly and clearly for all.

That fall dad leased a dryland farm three miles south of Conrad, Montana. He put in a winter crop there and seeded spring crops on the irrigation place. Jim got married and came to live with us that winter. In the spring he moved to the dryland place and he managed the irrigation place; by then it seemed the country was returning to its productive times.

Dad had a three year lease on the irrigation place. So when the lease was up, Jim renewed the lease for only one more year, as his heart was with the flour mills. When the year was up, he returned to live in Glasgow, Montana, and his love.

ESSEX STORYTELLER

Our oldest brother Matt just loved to tell Essex stories to anyone who would listen to him. Once he got a listener under the spell of his web—well—time meant nothing. All he had to do was say, how would you like to hear a story? We would gather around him with excitement.

"Now simmer down, so I can start!" he'd say.

Grinning from ear to ear, he was in the height of his glory when he could hold his audience's attention. I was hardly considered a child, but I still loved to hear them, especially with such a dramatic a speaker as he was. Many times dad would come up to the room and ask him to end it, as it was past our bedtime. We all clamored for one more, which pleased Matt.

"Have you forgotten that your wife is downstairs waiting; besides your little ones should be in their own beds?" dad said.

Matt looked sheepishly at his three sleepy heads and said,

"You are right, dad."

He picked them out of our beds, as we were in bed all ready, just lying there listening to the storyteller. The lights were blown out, as there was no sleeping in on the farm at any time unless you were ill, or a small child.

Matt and his family lived five miles from our place, so we got together often on weekends. Since he was the oldest of the children, he felt he could correct us, or criticize us like his own on what we wore, or how we looked if it was not to his liking, or approval. If father thought he was overly critical, he'd remind him who the parent was. Father didn't disapprove of short sleeves, or sleeveless dresses, or a little powder on one's face. Well, all this did not set very well with

Matt. He'd lower his face and walk away mumbling,

"They are getting older."

Matt meant sister Raya and me, but dad never neglected his part of devoted parent. Now this storyteller's wife (Paraska) believed in raising a garden, not just a plot, but five acres. When it came to keeping the weeds down, it seemed I was the easiest to bend for a helping hand. The weeding was done by hand and the nice juicy suckling were gathered and fed to the pigs and some to the cattle.

The garden hoe was used to loosen the dirt and to bank up the rows around the vegetables. Paraska asked mother for help that day, as she had to bake and clean house, so she said. Good old mother never refused help to any call of duty. Why should she, there was no back talk in those days.

"Frasinia, get ready to help Paraska with her garden weeding." she called out to me.

"But mother what about ours? I was going to work on it today; it certainly needs it."

"That is all right; you can work on it tomorrow," she said.

"Your father is going up that way to get some water while the irrigation ditch is filling in."

I was thinking to myself— good thing my folks only put in one acre of garden. Sad don't you think? I could be up to my armpits in weeds and at times I was. Nice thing about it at home, I had help— Raya and sometimes Maurice and George. The folks planted an acre of potatoes in the field. There, everybody took turns cultivating who was not busy at the time it had to be done.

"Frasinia are you ready to come with me?" dad called.

"I'm coming, dad!"

I ran out looking like a scarecrow except the straw was missing. I had on Bill's bib overalls, long sleeve shirt, lace up shoes and straw hat. Now, the reason I did not have my own such clothes was because girls didn't wear such clothes—maybe it was just us girls; at least it was not bought for us. Good thing we had brothers. Besides it helped to discourage the mosquitoes from trying to drain blood from oversized clothes.

When dad saw me, he smiled and helped me up to the top of the flat water tank. He took up the reins. The horses started to trot rather fast, which bounced me about the top causing a pain in my side. I crawled up to the front and sat beside dad. He smiled at me and noticed my pale face.

"Are you ill?" he asked. "Frasinia if you don't want to go, just say so; your mother is so big hearted with her children."

"Oh no, dad, I just got pain in my side bouncing about while the horses were trotting. It's getting better now. I'll be fine."

Dad had always been concerned about me. I was twenty pounds underweight and for a seventeen-year old and 5' 3" tall, I may have had a scarecrow resemblance with long golden hair and green eyes. My dad! How lucky I was—I thought to myself, as we smiled at each other. He was a man of great compassion for his family and fellow men, but wise as to any foolishness, or unjust action. That he would not tolerate and he would let one know without much hesitation.

When we got to Matt's place, I went directly to Paraska to get assigned to my place of duty. She told me to take a hoe and work on the potatoes. Her daughter Duna who was ten and a half years old at the time was to go with me and pull weeds while I banked up the potato rows. She was a sweet child with auburn hair, dancing brown eyes and beautiful white teeth. She was delighted to go with me, as this relieved her from babysitting. This was our day of freedom. This may sound strange to you. We were all alone and still doing the work. If she got behind in her weeding, I'd help out without any comment and we laughed freely without someone asking us to stop it and get busy. Her parents were stricter that way. Ours usually asked what was so funny.

Paraska sent down some piroshki and milk for our lunch with Duna's brother George. George was nine years old. He was a handsome lad, curly blonde hair and green eyes and with the most fetching smile. We saw him running across the field jumping over obstacles in his way.

"Piroshki are still hot and boy they are good—with new cabbage, tomatoes, onions and green peppers," he called out.

And they certainly were. We sat down beside a pile of weeds that was piled up and enjoyed our hearty lunch. George ate his lunch with us. He had been helping his brother Jack pick rocks off the field where their father Matt was plowing.

"I am supposed to tell mama how much work you have done," George said before he turned to leave.

"Go ahead!" we said laughing.

As it happened with all our freedom, we did remarkably well. We learned what work was when we were quite young. As the sun set, Duna and I started towards her house. She took my hand and said,

"Aunty Frasinia, I hope you will come back tomorrow; we had so much fun today."

"We sure did, Duna, but the folks may have other plans for us tomorrow."

Since it was late, Matt and his family drove me home after supper. Paraska took a bunch of fresh vegetables and a loaf of bread to mother. Although we had plenty of our own, I suppose it was considered my day's earnings. We never questioned wages at all. It was just helping each other when we were asked, or if we were able to. Before Matt left he told us another of his Essex stories, which made our day. He was so dramatic in his storytelling, that he lived it. God rest his soul.

We went to bed as soon as all the chores were done, as morning would come all too soon. Summer months found us stirring about 4 a.m.—so much had to be done to take in the abundance of God's gifts to us.

COOKING OUT

My father had one of the first threshing rigs in that community, so he was kept busy by the wheat growers. My job was to cook for his help. It was fun going out with him to different farms. I was taught to cook at the early age of eleven, so I thought I was a well seasoned cook at the age of seventeen.

Now cooking out is just like it sounds. Daddy would make a cooking vessel out in the open, by digging out a hole in the ground and placing a large grill over it. At one end it was dug out lower so I could feed the fire. Meals prepared on it were the kind that stuck to a man's ribs—potatoes, steak, salad, vegetables, coffee, bread and dessert. The men working for dad looked forward to them.

"We like to put our feet under Mr. Letz's table and get some of Frasinia's cooking," they would say.

Whether they meant it or not, they sure knew how to flatter a young girl's ego. As we moved from farm to farm, dad always came in just a bit earlier to help set up the table, which consisted of three wooden horse legs and long boards to create a long table; wooden benches were then placed on both sides for sitting, and the heavenly blue sky became the roof.

A fire was built and dinner started. The aroma of the cooking food filled the air and brought eager eaters to the table, but not before washing up in a basin which was filled with water from a bucket on hand and plenty of towels. There were at least six to eight extra men besides four of my brothers helping dad. Such a pleasant bunch, laughing and kidding each other—but with dad's watchful eye and keen ear, nothing out of order was said.

After being out for a couple of weeks, we went home for the

weekend and that week my brother Nick's sweetheart came over to spend a couple weeks with us on the farm. So the following Monday she came along with us for the rest of the harvesting—threshing. With her being there dad did not come in earlier to set up the tables. We managed very well by ourselves. She was a lovely person and a beauty—dark brown curly hair and face of an angel. (After harvesting Nick and Julia got married and Mike and I stood up for them.) Threshing was over for the year, and dad decided we should all go into town and have a meal. I think he wanted to give a treat to us cooks. It was fun—something special—those days for us. It thrills me now each time I think—what a lucky girl I was to have had such wonderful parents.

My father was the most kind and gentle and mother firm but loving and understanding. They both were rare and wonderful parents. Even now that they are gone I never feel alone. Mother lived for several years longer after dad passed away. I lived next door to mother and when I would come to see her, I'd find her in tears. I'd ask her why she was crying so much and she would say,

"If I had chosen to live my life over again, I'd want to live it just as it was."

"But mother," I'd say, "You said, there was so much rough times."

"Oh, I know—but dad and I made it anyway."

"Don't worry about me, Frasinia. It relieves me to cry. I miss your father."

And then she'd smile as she proceeded to relay her dream to me.

"Father is building a home for me on top of a hill. He said he is lonely for me and wants me to come soon. I told him I wanted an indoor bathroom, and he said he would do that for me."

I think that it thrilled her to think that she had not lost him at all even after death. A few days later she said that she dreamed of him again and he had everything ready, but again she put him off saying that the children still needed her. This made him very sad but said he'd wait for her. It seemed that mother enjoyed being with dad if only in her dreams. It made her more content with life in general until she was ready to join him. They are both gone now, but not forgotten.

FIRST DATE

My first date and four others—well, three couples is a nice crowd. On this big eventful day in my life, I was pulling weeds in the garden and dressed for the part, mostly to discourage the mosquitoes. I had on Bill's bib overalls, long sleeve shirt, high top shoes and a straw hat. Since I had been working quite a few hours, I looked up at the sun and it indicated lunch time. So I let myself out of the gate to go to the house and, as usual, the three little piglets were waiting for their lunch too. When they were born their mother could not feed so many, so these three piglets were bottle fed.

Since they knew no other mother, we did just fine. They followed us around every time we came out into the yard. Even when company was there they'd be right there with their snouts up in the air making pig noises. Most of the time people would stoop down and pat them. I guess they thought they were people. They started to follow me to the house, so I ran to get ahead of them otherwise they would walk into the house with me.

All three were looking through the screen door while I was preparing their lunch. I took their lunch to the pig shed in hopes they would get the drift where they belonged. Now, for my lunch, with the first fresh garlic from the garden I pulled out, I made myself a sandwich, bowl of yogurt, and a slice of salt pork. I had not been eating very long before there was a knock on the door. I went to answer it. Who should be there, but our neighbor's son Clifford; smiling he said,

"Hello!"

"Hello," I said.

"If you want to see Bill, he is out in the field," I continued.

"No, I don't want to see Bill; I came to see you."

"Me, I asked. Why?"

"I want to know if you will go to the dance with me this Saturday at Ledger."

"I'll have to ask mother," I said.

Mother had been taking this in and smiled when I asked her.

"I am sure that it will be just fine, since Bill, Raya and their friends will be going along," she said.

The young man had no choice—but to agree. He left still smiling. We had been going this way for a long time—the six of us, and he wanted me to go alone with him. Now, his impression of me that day was not very flattering. It proved itself out when he came with his sister to pick all of us up. I noticed his onion breath. Still it did not register to me until we were dancing. He started to laugh and said,

"I am sorry. I'll have to get some gum. I ate onions to protect myself."

Then it dawned on me. Oh, my garlic sandwich. I blushed easily those days. I was more careful of my diet thereafter.

We had a joyful summer—the six of us—horseback riding, picnics, and ice-cream socials. Just before we were to move to city life, his folks invited us to dinner. The day was filled with many events—horseback riding the earlier part of the day, a horseshoe game, then to a wonderful chicken dinner. Clifford's mother had fresh onions on the table, so there was more teasing about the garlic. We had onions that day just the same. After dinner we settled down to a game of cards, which lasted later than we had planned. When we got home, dad and mother thought we carried the good thing a bit too late.

That fall dad and mother retired to city life with the five youngest children. Bill was 19, Raya 15, Maurice 13, George 11, and I was 17 years old. With school starting in a couple weeks, the move was not delayed. We found ourselves in the city of Great Falls, Montana. Now, we had been quite a close knit five-sum. The city life changed that in a very short time. Maurice and George faced the jungle of city life. Their situation was most devastating to their pride the first day of school on the way home. It seemed a group of boys got hold of them and lowered their pants and spat on their bare bottoms. Well, this was carrying it too far, much too far as far as the boys were concerned. I overheard this by chance when they were plotting how they would get even with those boys. How they would get each one alone as time and place permitted. You can rest assured this was carried out.

I took time out to listen to their progress when I would hear or see them huddled together—planning and giggling in some corner, or back of a building—sometimes nursing a scratch, or a bruise bravely, like some sort of medal of honor. I noticed before long they were a close two-sum, more than ever before, but it paid off. They were respected even by the larger boys in the neighborhood.

Raya was going to commercial college taking up business courses—shorthand and typing. Bill got a job on a sheep ranch for the winter months. Dad was too much a country man; he just could not retire to "ideal life" as he called it. So dad leased some land on shares, not too far from Great Falls, and commuted back and forth home. In the early spring Bill helped dad with the work. When school was out, Maurice and George joined the two on the farm. Sometimes they batched in a shack on the place, so as not to lose valuable time. Time is the secret of good farming. Mother was keeping the home fire burning with expert hands. She had a garden planted and a well balanced budget. I usually shopped for mother on my day off from work.

A few blocks from home was a mercantile store owned by three brothers. They were of Austrian descent. When I'd come into their store they would call out,

"Hello, Frasinia! Shopping day for mother again?"

"Yes! I have an order to be filled."

After the order was filled, I'd browse around a bit, as their store had everything for ones need in one stop shopping. Walking past a cheese counter, I had thought I found some spoiled cheese—molded badly.

"Mr. Anthoneo, do you realize you have some spoiled cheese in the case?" I said.

"Frasinia, it is not spoiled—that is one of our best sellers," he said and laughed.

Then he went on to explain the names of different cheeses and their processes. I told him the only cheese we enjoyed was what mother made—cottage cheese, sweet milk cheese with a pill added to it, and yogurt. We enjoyed many delicious foods made from the good wholesome milk. As I picked up the rest of the groceries, Mr. Anthoneo spoke in a questioning manner,

"Frasinia, What I want to know is how your mother manages to feed a family of seven on $87 for three months?"

"Why, we even have company quite often," I said smiling.

"It's a good thing we do not have too many of those budgeters, or we'd go broke."

As I was walking out of the store, a young man was coming in. He held the door open for me and said,

"You're Maurice and George's sister, aren't you?"

Since I was a very naive person at that time in my life, I answered,

"Yes!"

I thanked him for holding the door open for me and walked on.

That evening my two little brothers approached me with eyes wide open and smiling.

"Frasinia, there is a fellow that thinks you are beautiful and he'd like a date with you," Maurice said.

"I don't know such a fellow," I said.

"Oh, he held the door open for you at the store today," Maurice said as George stood by to verify Maurice's statement.

"Gosh, you are pretty; we didn't know that," they said.

Well, to be truthful, I hadn't given much thought to it myself. I had to hear it a few times before I went to the mirror to check it out. Far as our family went, we were all normal and handsome people. So

I never had to compare, or even thought about it. We were praised for our deeds and not for our looks. Somehow it never entered our mind to run to our parents and say you don't love me. We just knew we were loved. I guess it was because of security and consistency of their devotion through the years that kept us reasonably balanced through trying times. It was not as if we did not have trauma in our lives, we just did not throw in the towel, so to speak, but we tried to work it out for the best, or accepted it and prayed it would work out. As a rule nothing was ever so hopeless that it didn't have some sort of reason for showing its ugly head before we could see the bright side again. My brothers were waiting for my answer.

"My answer is NO! If he wants a date with me, he will have to ask me himself."

"In about an hour," I answered as the boys asked when dinner would be ready.

They ran outside. I wondered what was going on in their mind for future plans. Mother was hanging out the clothes and I started to prepare dinner.

"I just met my future son-in-law," mother said as she came in smiling.

"For whom mother?" I asked.

After all, Raya was around too. I laughed and went about my work. Mother kept on talking,

"He said hello, bowed, and tipped his cap; now this is always a good sign of any young man's intentions."

"What does he look like, mother?"

"Oh, blonde, blue eyes, about 6-feet and has a nice smile. I saw him walk up to the big house on the corner," she said. "I have often seen him walk through the alley up that way. He must come off the street car from work."

Mother enjoyed being outside talking with neighbors over the fence to find out just a bit of what happened that day.

"Mother, how about me changing jobs with you?" I asked.

She laughed with a twinkle in her eyes and went to check the boiling pot to see what I was cooking. Then I told her about what Maurice and George asked of me. Mother just laughed and said,

"Now, don't be talked into any—blind dates."

"No mother, I will not."

After dinner was over, my brother Arrsum sent Lenna, his daughter, over to ask Raya and me to come over for a while and visit them. (He had quit farming a few years before dad did and started to work for the Smelter Company. They moved into a house dad owned right next to us). Not knowing what he wanted, we went there with Lenna. When we walked in Liza and Arrsum smiled at us and asked us to meet Arthur Landgren, who happened to have stopped to visit them. Arrsum met him through the work at the Smelter.

After our introduction, I realized who the man was through mother's description of him. He did have beautiful blonde curly hair, but I was not impressed with him, as he made me very uncomfortable by staring at me. I tried hiding back of the big coal heater that was in most homes in those days.

"Sis, why don't you come here and sit by Liza? I can't see you back there," Arrsum said.

He was smiling at me. I blushed with embarrassment and said in Russian,

"I'm going home!"

"He is a nice young man from a good family. He wants to meet you."

I noticed Raya was enjoying herself, laughing and talking with Lenna.

"Raya let's go home, I said. Mother has things for us to do yet."

We left after a polite goodnight. The following weekend mother informed me that Raya, I, and she were invited for lunch at Mrs. Landgren's home. This was not my idea of a pleasant time—remembering only too well our last meeting.

"Is her son going to be there?" I asked.

"I don't know Frasinia," she answered.

When we arrived there his mother was a most gracious person. (What else could the poor mother do—but to follow her son's wishes?) They had a lovely three story home, beautifully furnished. We sat down and had lunch. It was well prepared and tasty. Just before we left, Arthur came home from work tipsy and he looked at me smiling.

"I like you and I hope you will like me too."

I blushed, and thought to myself, never, I don't like a drinking man. (I had been negatively impressed with my sister Mary's husband and his abusive way to her when he drank and that left a mark on me.)

"Don't tease her now. Go and clean up," his mother said.

"Okay mother! I'll be right back; now don't leave."

When he left, mother graciously said,

"Thank you very much for a lovely lunch. You girls stay and help Mrs. Landgren with the dishes."

"Oh, no!" she said, "I'll do them myself."

I, for one, was happy to get away. Raya followed without too much persuasion.

Without my knowledge, Arthur was weaving a web to catch me. He was a perfect gentleman. He was willing to be a foursome at anytime to go to a show, or dance, and he never made me feel closed in. I noticed he did not drink when he was around me. So I asked my little brothers if by chance they had something to do with it.

"Well, he asked us what he could do to make you like him and we told him to stop drinking. Honest sis. That is all we said."

"Is that how you got the .22 gun," I asked.

"We did not want to take it, but he said we really earned it. We heard you say that you don't like men that drink. Now, didn't you?"

"Yes, I did, but please don't let him bribe you anymore. Just tell him to ask me if he is in doubt about anything."

Arthur never tried kissing me at anytime. When Christmas came his brother Harry came home on his vacation from college. Bill,

Raya, and I went over to Landgren's on Christmas Eve to wish them a Merry Christmas and Mr. Landgren a happy birthday. They always celebrated that day we were told. We met Harry that evening. He was a pleasant man and handsome too; and he kept asking me questions,

"Are you my brother's girlfriend? Do you have other boyfriends?"

"I am no ones girlfriend," I said.

I really believed it to be so, that I was free as the breeze. Harry was a handsome man with straight blonde hair, blue eyes and a beautiful smile besides 6' 2" tall. So when he asked me for a date, well, I said, "Yes."

We went to the show that evening, believe it or not; a street car took us there and back. He was quite a gentleman, but not so slow in kissing me goodnight.

"Would you consider going to the New Years Eve dance with me," he asked.

I told him I'd think about it. What happened? I'll never know, but he never pressed me after that. His younger brother may have had a heart to heart talk with him, or it could have been that our farm day friends came to visit us during that time. Clifford tried his best to convince me of his love while he was there. I was kind and respected his feeling, but I could not return the same feeling for him. I liked him as a friend.

"I'll try not to rush you, Frasinia, but you think about what I said."

His sister Mildred came with him to visit us too. Bill and she had been friends, since that time Mildred fell in love with "a man of her heart's desire" she told Raya and me.

"Clifford wanted me to come; he thought it would look better," she said.

"Good for Clifford. We are happy to see you too," we both chimed at the same time.

It seemed that Arthur was always around—just unexpectedly.

Clifford noticed and asked me if Arthur was my boyfriend. It just never dawned on me, as he usually spent time talking with my brothers and once in awhile I was spoken to. So I laughed and said,

"I do not have a certain boyfriend."

"Maybe you think that, but he is in love with you," Clifford said.

The last evening they were with us, Harry, Arthur, Mildred, Clifford, Bill, Raya and me—we all took a hike to Giant Springs. It was five miles one way from our homes. We started walking on a path following the bank of the Missouri River. It was a lovely brisk evening. The snow crunched under our feet, as we walked along, laughing and talking. Clifford was holding my hand. Arthur walked on the other side of me. Harry, Mildred, Raya and Bill were walking single file, as the path narrowed. Clifford walked ahead still holding my hand.

As I laughingly tried to pull away, he only tightened the hold more, so I followed, blushing with embarrassment. Finally we reached Giant Springs. They are the largest fresh water springs in the world. The area was all lit up and very beautiful. We all enjoyed the sight and walk. Of course Harry and Arthur were able to enlighten us more as to its history, as they had lived in Black Eagle, Montana, for quite a few years. Black Eagle is a suburb just across the Missouri River from Great Falls and that is where we made our home too.

After coming home, the Landgren men bid us goodnight and walked on home. The rest of us decided to have hot chocolate and sweet rolls. As they were leaving by train early the next morning, Mildred said, "I think I'll turn in for the night!" Raya walked up the stairs with her and Bill went to his room. I started to follow the girls saying goodnight. Clifford asked if I'd just stay up a bit longer as he wished to talk to me. I sat down by the table across from him and he took hold of my hands.

"Do you realize how much I have missed you? Would you consider being my girlfriend? You did say you had no special boyfriend."

"I know, I did, Clifford, but I do not wish to give my pledge to anyone yet."

"Well, I won't rush you, but you will please think about it?"

I said that I would think about it and tried to leave again, but he drew me close and tried kissing me. I turned my face to avoid his lips touching mine. He kissed my check. With all the fun we had on the farm together, this was his first attempt and then I was shy. He pressed me to him and said,

"Goodnight and remember what I asked you."

I nodded my head and walked up the stairs to my room. I shared the same room with Raya and Mildred, so they both looked at me as I came in. Mildred knew why her brother wanted to make the trip to see me. She just smiled at me.

Next morning after breakfast the four of us drove to the depot and bid our friends farewell. As I was giving my hand to Clifford, he drew me to him and kissed my check, smiled and said,

"Now don't forget to think about it; I'll be waiting."

I promised that I would—and blushed as he kissed my check again.

"I like to make you blush. Write please," he said as Mildred called,

"Clifford, come on—or we'll miss the train."

We waved to them as the train pulled out. Bill was teasing me about Clifford. Raya was silent. I guess she had other thoughts in her head which weren't on his toasting.

One evening Harry came over to bid us goodbye, as his vacation came to an end. Since we did not get a chance to go dancing while he was home, he said,

"Don't forget we have a date when I come back home in June."

"Sure thing in June," I said and laughed.

He bid everyone goodbye and left. When everything settled down to normal again, my dad asked me how I would like to go to beauty school. I really had not given it a thought, but being a dutiful daughter I said,

"Yes dad if that is what you want me to do."

"No, it's not what I want, but I think you should have some sort of profession. I looked into it the other day and they are signing up a new class at the American Beauty School."

So I, Frasinia, was signed in for classes to become a beautician. Dad was a wise man and figured things were moving a bit too fast for his young daughter, so he decided on a worthy cause without too much explaining about life and its pitfalls. Anyway, I put my heart and soul into work. Dad and mother were pleased. I was kept so busy that I did not have time for boyfriends. The family got free haircuts and neighbors too. So kind of them to let me practice on their heads, even my silent admirer asked me to cut his hair. I didn't know that in a few years I'd have him for a steady customer. More than anything, I learned how to bring out my best features and step. Dad was pleased that his daughter was growing up. He was a great admirer of beauty and liked to see people culture it. And in his own way, he hoped his little chick would learn to culture her sleeping beauty.

It was most interesting, those months of school. I met lots of nice people. I passed my examination and again dad came forth with how would I like a shop of my own, which was not really the best idea, as my teacher informed me that I should work for her or some other beauty shop and build up my own clientele.

Well, I went ahead and got my shop. There was a barber shop and it had a balcony room which was used for a beauty shop at one time, so everything was there that was needed for twenty dollars a month. My business lasted as long as I thought it took to be profitable. In the first place, it was in the wrong place, and in the second place, my teacher was right.

I was in the post office one morning and the postmaster asked me,

"Frasinia, do you still have your shop downtown?"

"No I do not," I said.

"Would you like to try it here in Black Eagle? I have a room in this building and it was used for a beauty shop before. It did a good business. The woman that had it got sick and had to stop working. You can have it for fifteen dollars a month."

"Why, thank you. I'll ask my folks about it this evening and let you know in the morning."

Next morning I went there with the first month's rent. It was all settled and I moved in. The business was much better, but something was not just right. So I asked Mr. Kovich what could be the matter. He said that he heard that Mary had started working in her home since she got well. It could be the reason, as she had a big following. This was a close knit Italian society.

I realized I made the mistake of stepping on their toes. I was not of their religion, or race. I learned more about this as time went by. Finally my beauty career was coming to an end. The ladies that came to me did not come back and I could not make a living just cutting hair off the heads of my own family. There were a few other nationalities in Black Eagle—like Slovaks, Czechs, few Swedes and Russians. We were the minor minority. They made us welcome and for that our world was brighter.

I merely made expenses. One day I was planning on giving it up, as a young woman came into my shop and said,

"I am Mary. You probably heard about me. I had this place for quite a few years and had to quit because I got sick. I am fine now and I'd like to have this place back. I have been quite busy in our home, and my family isn't happy about it. It makes our home life a bit too hectic."

I sympathized with her, but an idea was weaving in my mind. I asked her if she would consider coming in with me and we both could build up a nice business.

"I don't think it would work." she said.

"Why do you say that?"

"Well, you are not of our nationality," she said.

"Why should that make a difference," I said. "You are a Czech?"

"I married one of the Italian boys and joined their church; if I went into business with you, we'd both lose out," she continued.

"Oh, I see. Thank you for explaining to me. Now I know why the lack of business here."

She was a beautiful girl. As a child she had polio and it left her with one leg crippled which was very noticeable. Although she was able to use it by swinging her hip to help her leg move forward to walk, she was quite bent over to one side because of the shorter limb. After she left it was almost closing time. I started to straighten the place, and who should come in—but Uncle Steve. We called him that just to be respectful of our elders. Uncle Steve had other plans for me. He had been pestering my folks for my hand in marriage. My folks told him I was too young for him, and I was.

"Hello, Uncle Steve," I said.

"Stop calling me Uncle Steve. I am really not your uncle," he said.

Knowing what he was leading up to I said,

"Oh, but as far as I am concerned, you will always be my Uncle Steve."

"Frasinia, will you give me a facial pack?"

"Oh, sure if that's what you want!" thinking to myself—that should keep him from talking for awhile.

I told him to sit down in the chair and I put some hot towels on his face first. He asked me if that was necessary.

"Yes, I have to open up the pores and then the pack will go on."

Finally the pack was put on. I informed him that at no time must he speak while it was drying otherwise it would not do the job. I let him look into the hand mirror once in awhile to see how it was drying. The poor man thought it would remove the few wrinkles he had. He really was a fine looking man and I liked him, but only as an uncle. He had been a friend of the family for a long time. This is not the first time that he tried to get into the family. Olga was his first and she was too young by my folks' standard point of view on age difference.

The postmaster must have been taking in the conversion, so he called me. I excused myself and went to see what he wanted.

"Is that man bothering you?" he asked.

"No—not really. You must have heard us talk."

"Yes, so he wants to marry you," he said with a twinkle in his eye.

I blushed and went back to my work. Uncle Steve's face was ready to have the pack removed. I told him I had to put more packs on his face to remove the mask. When I got through with him, his face was nice and pink. I don't think he ever had so much work done before on his face. After the pack was removed I gave him a good facial massage with cream and then more ice packs. While this was going on, I warned him not to talk, because I could get some cream in his mouth.

Poor uncle had so much to talk about and the time was wrong. After that, I had to close up because it was past closing time for the owner and I didn't have my own door to leave by. On the way home Steve asked me if I thought his face looked younger.

"You don't look old and you certainly have not a thing to worry about."

"Then, why don't you marry me? I'll be good to you."

"Uncle Steve, I am not ready for marriage, and you know my folks don't want me to."

That evening he told my folks, since he could not marry into our family he would never get married. The folks told him that they were sure he would find a fine lady that he would love someday. Next day he left for his home. The folks heard from him a few times since then, but as far as we knew he was still a bachelor.

That evening I told my folks about my work. It was not the end of the world they informed me, after all they were sure I could get a job soon. So the next morning I told my landlord that I was giving up the place.

"Frasinia, I couldn't help but overhear what Mary said to you yesterday and I'll never rent the place to her. I'll just use it for a storage room first," he said.

"You really don't have to take it out on her," I said.

"Oh, I know, but they have been running this Black Eagle too much."

"They just may stop buying from you." I said.

"Don't worry about it; it is only a side business and I have been here a long time."

He was a Slovak. Since there was only one post office in Black Eagle and he was running it, they all came to it. He had a small grocery store—which was handy when one ran out of a few articles—something like Circle K only smaller.

He certainly kept his word to me. Whenever I went to the post office, or to shop, I noticed the room was used for storage. Mary did her business in her home and then later on I saw her working in a beauty salon in Great Falls.

After my eighteenth birthday in the year of 1928, I got a job—housework—for Mrs. Birch. Mr. Birch was a big contractor in Montana and they had their home in Great Falls. I must have pleased her for she complimented me on my work. How could I fail with a mother, like mine, that believed in an early start in life's work?

HOUSEWORK

I had never worked in such a modern home—so many rooms to keep clean and everything on schedule. Breakfast was served at 5:00 a.m. sharp, lunch 12:00 noon and dinner at 6:00 p.m.—which wasn't unusual for me as I had done this before, except at home I had help, but here everything had to be done by me. I learned how to serve at the table, and how to take afternoon naps to gain strength—something we did not do at home, unless we were ill. Our home style was placing the food on the table and everybody passed it around. My monthly income was $45 and with board and room.

After I had been there a few months, she raised my wages to $50—big deal—as I told her daughter. Mr. Birch had gotten a big contracting job, so she told her mother what I had said. Mrs. Birch just smiled at me later in the day when she finally got around to it.

"Frasinia, soon as Mr. Birch gets some of that money, I'll raise your wages."

"Thank you!" I said as I looked at her and turned back to do the dishes.

Mrs. Birch was a kind and patient woman. She taught me to prepare many unusual American dishes for meals and many other social etiquettes which I value more now than the wages then. They were all very kind to me, of course the children played less pranks, but we all did at one time or another. I liked the family.

When school was out, we all drove up to their cabin by King's Hill in the mountains. It was a lovely place. Mrs. Birch and I cleaned the place and rearranged the cupboards and put groceries away. Then I got busy and prepared the dinner, as Mr. Birch was coming for the weekend. We stayed there all summer until school started in the fall.

During the summer, I went on hikes with the children and waded in the mountain stream. The family went swimming together in the river, but as for me, I just waded. I couldn't swim, besides—I had no bathing suit. I climbed trees, more those days, that was my passion, or so it seemed. I could see more of the world from them.

Arthur Landgren spent his two weeks vacation close by in a tent. He brought Maurice, George, and Beverly (his friend's son) with him. Now, I did not know of this, until Maurice and George came up to the cabin to see me one morning and told me that they were all there camping. They wanted to know when I could come and see them.

"I will when I have free time," I said.

Mrs. Birch was taking it all in, smiled at me with a twinkle in her eyes and asked if he was my boyfriend. I immediately denied that and said,

"Oh, no, just a family friend."

I introduced my brothers to her. She told them I would be free to go see them after I was through with my duties. They left for their camp. I could see they were anxious to tell me something more.

The bib overalls were stylish at that time. Mrs. Birch allowed me to use them on weekdays while we were there. I had to be fresh and clean at all times while cooking and serving. I really felt more comfortable in dresses, or uniforms.

After my duties were over, I slipped into a shirt and bib overalls to go visit them. They located themselves just across from a grove of tall pine trees out of the view from the main highway and the cabin. Arthur was brewing coffee and had some of his mother's homemade pineapple filled rolls. The coffee aroma was filling the cool air with its fragrance; Arthur smiled at me and said,

"Welcome to this humble setting. The boys thought it would be fun to camp out. They told me that they had never camped out in their whole life. Your folks were pleased about it; hope you don't mind."

"Why should I mind? It is very kind of you to bother with my brothers, and I am sure they'll have a ball."

The boys were grinning at me mischievously, as if they had a big secret, which I am sure they did, but I wasn't going to pry, but wait until it got to be too much for them and it would spill out soon. I sat down on the ground and Arthur handed me a cup of coffee and a roll. M-m-m! It was tasty.

They started to tell me about setting up the tent in the dark, as it was quite late when they drove up. Besides it started to sprinkle. By the time the tent was set up they were damp and chilly. Once bedded down they were lulled to sleep by the steady drizzling rain.

Morning found the boys scurrying for their clothes as the aroma of breakfast cooking spiked their hunger more. They settled around the warm fire with plates and food and a hot cup of cocoa. This was told to me later by Maurice.

The sun was already up in the sky, drying the earth and warming the drowsy insects, before I got around to visiting them after my morning duties. It was amusing the way they clamored about me to tell me what took place, laughing and the boys talking at the same time. Arthur just smiled at them and kept glancing up at me now and then, perhaps to see how I was taking it all.

"Oh," he said, "I brought a camera with me. Frasinia, how about having your picture taken with the boys?"

Maurice sauntered by and the picture was taken; then Maurice said,

"How about one of you with Arthur?"

"I really have to go now and make lunch," I said.

I thanked Arthur for the coffee and the roll. As I was leaving they all got up and walked with me across the road to the cabin.

"When can we see you again?" George asked.

"I'll come whenever I can," I said—waving goodbye, and I walked into the house.

"Frasinia, you had quite an escort," smiled Mrs. Birch.

I noticed that her three children were unhappy with me.

"What's the matter?" I asked them.

"Why didn't you take us with you?" they asked.

"I'm sorry. I had no idea you wanted to go, and if it's all right with your mother, why it is all right with me."

"We did, we did!" all three chimed in.

"I didn't think you would want them on your time off, Frasinia," Mrs. Birch said.

"Oh, I don't mind, if you don't. I am sure they will be delighted to have extra guests. If Arthur can stand three boys on his vacation for two weeks—three more should be that much more fun."

"He sure must love children—that family friend; I'd like to meet him," she said and laughed.

I was into the spirit of the discussion by now, and laughingly said,

"Anytime."

Her children had me to themselves before these invaders came and that didn't set too well with the children. Our first get together wasn't until after lunch the next day. (I must explain about the children—Martha was the oldest. She was 12-years old, taller than I, and she made me aware of her in her own little way. Judith the 10-year old was of average size, very sweet and a thoughtful child. Steven was 8-years old with a big little boy crush on me.)

As we were walking into their camp, the boys were in the process of cleaning their catch of fish. The boys, overly zealous about their fishing trip, made my three little companions feel slighted.

"Wait, wait, boys, I want you to meet some very fine friends of mine," I called out.

After the introductions, things eased up some as the boys and Arthur took over being hosts in one grand way—another angle of approach, don't you agree? But I was very pleased. It certainly helped to relax the three guests. Arthur built a fire and we all ate around it and exchanged small talk and laughed. He made hot cocoa for all of us and served it with cookies. His dear mother must have spent a few of her precious busy hours getting things ready for her son's vacation and his friends', friends, putting it mildly; they were like fleas on a dog. He had won them over completely. He was a fine person; I can't blame the boys. Eventually I realized that he was a man of integrity; I just didn't like the idea of being fenced in. I was just beginning to realize there was more to the world than our backyard. I knew it was beautiful, but so much more exciting now. So I was always looking out for signs. Oh, you might even call me suspicious—the little games that went on between Arthur and the boys, perhaps to silence them to their agreement with him. Anyway, I thought he was a good campaigner in his own silent way.

As we had planned to gather wildflowers for the cabin, we took leave and walked up the slope of the hill spilling over with colors you could hardly imagine. Maurice, George, and Beverly came along with us. Arthur stayed at the camp. With armfuls of lovely spring boughs of wildflowers, we started walking towards the cabin. Just before we got there, Arthur met us and handed me a bouquet.

"I gathered them close by the campsite, he said."

"Why, thank you," I said. I am sure Mrs. Birch will be happy to have more flowers."

"Oh, But I want you to have them," he said smiling.

I blushed more wildly than the wildflowers, as I thanked him again. You can rest assured the youthful audience missed nothing. I felt the silence of Martha as she and the others followed me home. Mrs. Birch watched our coming through the window and met us in the kitchen as we walked in. She noticed that my bouquet was arranged nicely already and said,

"We'll put that bouquet in the living room," to which Martha objected,

"Arthur gave them to Frasinia."

(If you haven't been around that part of Montana, you have missed the most glorious of God's setting for people. I can't begin to describe the beauty of different flowers in bloom covering the sloping hills, different trees putting on their green robes and grass pushing

its way amongst everything.

In our hikes, we'd drop onto the lush sloping hillsides and roll down to the bottom of the valley filled with more of the same beauty. Mrs. Birch's children joined us many times on hikes and fishing trips. They would be bubbling over with excitement when we'd return from one of those outings. It pleased Mr. and Mrs. Birch.)

"Then Frasinia should put them in her bedroom," she said.

"Mrs. Birch, I don't mind if you want them in the living room—really!"

"Here, put your flowers in this vase and take them into your bedroom, Frasinia."

I was happy when this flower business was over with. Next day it rained so hard I never stuck my nose out of the cabin. It was on the afternoon of the following day that I looked out of the window and saw Mrs. Birch talking with Arthur and the three boys. They were smiling at one another and then Arthur tipped his cap to her and all four walked on down the road. I turned quickly away from the window and started to busy myself with the housework. When she came inside, she smiled at me and said,

"I had the pleasure of meeting your folks' friend and Beverly, too. They missed you and wondered if you were ill. I told them that you'd see them soon. Frasinia, your brothers seemed anxious to see you too. You are just about through aren't you? Why don't you take a walk with them; I am sure you can catch up if you hurry. You can finish the rest of the work later. I am going to drive to a grocery store not far from here and take the children with me."

"Thank you, Mrs. Birch; I won't be gone too long."

I ran down the road where I had seen them go and found them sitting on a fallen log waiting for me. Great, such conspiracy, I thought.

"You're working for quite a nice lady, Frasinia," Arthur said.

I pretended I knew nothing of what took place before.

"Oh, I see you finally have met her," I said. "Yes, she is a very considerate person."

"Yes, we went past the cabin this morning and she was out in the yard. It was nice of her to let you come so soon. Our vacation is coming to an end and I thought maybe we could have a few pictures taken so the boys have something to remember the place they camped."

"Fine, let's start, as I really don't have that much time today."

We passed a big boulder and I said,

"Why don't you sit on it Arthur and we'll take your picture?"

Maurice took his picture sitting on it. I walked ahead and was leaning against a big tree with my arms about it laughing. Before I became aware of what was taking place, Arthur had a hold of my hand and the picture was snapped. It was quite a joke on me; the boys became quite hysterical about how it all turned out. Well, at least it awakened me to the fact that Arthur wasn't really playing a game with me. What should I do? I thought. Perhaps I better not go there anymore. My feelings were so mixed up for him. I liked him very much, but I thought there was more, or had heard of it. I smiled and bid bye-bye to them and started to run back to the cabin, as I did not wish any company escorting me that day.

The following Saturday evening Mrs. Birch told Mr. Birch about how she met Arthur and the rest of the boys.

"Frasinia tells me that he is a friend of the family, but I don't think he thinks that way."

Of course I was tensed about it; then Martha said,

"He just looks at her all the time when we are together."

That evening while I was doing the dishes, Steven came into the kitchen to ask me if he was still my boyfriend.

"You know, Frasinia, I love you, and you do love me, don't you?"

I reassured him that all was well with us. He was happily about to help with drying the dishes, when his mother came and shooed him out, so I could finish my work. As the next day was Sunday and the two weeks were up, the boys and Arthur came by to bid us all goodbye.

The summer months went by fast and school was just a week away. We started packing and getting ready to leave for their home in Great Falls, Montana, in a few days.

When we got back, it barely seemed that we entered the house when the telephone rang. It was for me from Arthur asking when he could see me. Since it was Friday evening, Mrs. Birch told me I could have Sunday off and be back for Monday morning. I told him I'd be home Sunday. It seemed that he had been calling there for the past week to find out if we were back.

"We just may lose Frasinia before long. He sure is an attentive young man," Mr. Birch told Mrs. Birch.

I guess my indifferent attitude made them aware my feeling was not the same, at least for the present. Saturday evening they drove me home. As I thanked them for bringing me home, Mrs. Birch said,

"Perhaps it would be better for you to come back tomorrow evening, as Monday you have to wake up so early." I promised to, as I waved goodbye to them.

It was like a family reunion—Arthur was there with my family members. I was happy to see my parents as I had not seen them all summer long—so many questions were asked and I hope answered to their satisfaction. The evening was joyfully spent. Arthur left before midnight, as he had to work that evening. Unbeknownst to me, it had been arranged so he could have a day off when I was home. I found that out the next day.

I got up early to have a longer day with my family. I was on the way to the kitchen where I heard mother's voice, but I was interrupted by voices coming from outside. I stopped and looked through the glass curtained window. Dad and Arthur were laughing and talking, standing on the sidewalk in front of our home. Mother called out that breakfast was ready from the kitchen, as the living room door was open. I was observing the play that was going on; dad must have asked Arthur to come in and have breakfast with us. He seemed to be declining, then—well, maybe a cup of coffee; anyway he was following dad inside. I rushed into the kitchen to help mother; I really didn't want to be caught spying on them, so I acted surprised when Arthur greeted me with

"Good Morning!" and a smile, "My, you are an early riser."

"But not as early as you," I smiled back.

We all sat down to breakfast. Arthur was persuaded to have breakfast, too. After it was over, I went into the kitchen to do the dishes—one guess as to my helper that blessed Sunday morning?

"Frasinia, where is the dishtowel? I'll help you wipe the dishes while you wash."

"Oh, no—Arthur, you go and talk with the men; the girls can do them alone," mother said.

"I can do that anytime, Mrs. Letz," he said, laughing.

Mother smiled and left to talk with father. Maurice and George went out to play with a couple of their friends, and as for Bill, he had a heavy date, as he voiced it, with a gal across the street to go horseback riding. Raya was making up the beds. Arthur was making small talk, and then he said,

"Frasinia, mother would like you to have dinner with us this evening. After that I'll take you back to the Birch's, if you'll let me."

"I'll have to ask mother; she may have other plans for me."

"I'll ask her," he said, leaving for the living room.

"It's fine with your parents, Frasinia," he said as he returned smiling.

Just then, Raya was walking into the kitchen asking me what I was going to be doing that afternoon.

"I want to go see a movie, but I can't go alone. I sure hope you can go with me."

"Why I'll be happy to take both of you to the show," Arthur responded after taking it all in.

He didn't bargain on Maurice and George, too. But that was exactly what he ended up with—three more than he bargained for—poor fellow. He realized he was courting the whole family, but that did not weaken his set goal. Father offered to pay for three of the children, but Arthur declined graciously.

When we got to the theater, the ticket taker knew us children and she smiled at me and winked. It was so funny. By the time we settled down, Arthur almost missed sitting by us. He had to ask the boys if they would mind if he sat next to me. Raya was on one side of me and the boys sat to Arthur's right side. I looked at him while he was trying to arrange this touchy situation. His face was very composed; he felt my look and turned his head and winked at me. I blushed most becomingly. He whispered to me as he finally sat down. I didn't turn to look at him, as I felt the whole theater looking at me.

The show was reviewed all the way home and then again to the folks by Maurice and George. Mother and dad laughed with the boys and their reliving the show. Then they ran outside, I suppose to tell it to their friends.

"Arthur, you made a couple boys very happy." my parents said.

It was a good dragged out show we all enjoyed, at least the ones that watched it. Raya and I left to get ready for dinner. Arthur went home to inform his mother that there would be an extra guest. The unexpected always happened to him. By now, I am sure his parents were not very surprised, besides they had enough food to feed a crew.

Raya and I were very close sisters and this third party was cramping our style. He sensed this and played according to our pleasure. He called up and asked if we'd mind walking up to the house alone. We were delighted as it was only a block and a half from our place, besides this gave us time to talk over our summer separation. So many things happened since we last saw each other. The few hours we had to ourselves just flew by and before we knew it, it was time to go. We walked hand-in-hand to the Landgren's place and were greeted by his father's booming, but jovial voice. Arthur was helping his mother place the food on the table. The evening was lovely and the dinner delicious. His mother was a great cook. His parents were such delightful and gracious hosts.

Arthur's father was a big man, 6' 4" tall and 240 pounds. His mother was very pleasant and a concerned mother, as most mothers are about their children. She had a good reason to be, from her point of view (I can understand it now), and her son had to please the whole family to have a few minutes with the apple of his eye. Well at least he'd have me alone that night on my return to my place of work.

After helping with the dishes and thanking them again, we left for home. I had to pick up my suitcase and bid my family goodbye. Arthur took the suitcase and helped me into the car. As we were going, I noticed he was not going straight to the Birch's, so I said,

"You are driving in the wrong direction."

"I know. I hope you don't mind. It's kind of early yet and I thought it would be nice to go for a ride."

"Well—just so we don't get back too late, as Monday morning comes too soon."

"I'll have you back before midnight," he smiled. "Do you realize we are alone for the first time?"

"Oh, I never mind being with a crowd."

I really meant it, but somehow it was not what he expected me to say. I was so sorry. I guess being around a large family and friends just did not enter my mind that it was a privilege to be alone with someone.

"I consider it so—to be with you," he laughed.

Blushing, I turned my face away. The ride was pleasant and conversation was kept light. It was 11 p.m. when he drove up to the Birch's home. He bid me goodnight and waited until I got inside. Four o'clock came around much too soon—it was Monday morning and wash day. I had the washing well on the way and breakfast served by 5:00 a.m.

I worked for Mrs. Birch until school was out, then I decided to get another job. I started to work as an usherette at Liberty Theatre six days a week. It was quite different from housework, and I never seemed to graduate from that; it was always waiting at home for me. I enjoyed meeting people, and of course seeing different shows made it interesting until it became part of the job. Another year went by in my life and my experiences all became part of growing up. We were adjusting to city life. It was quite different from country living, but as usual we adjusted easily in our youthful years.

Our first Christmas tree in America was furnished by Arthur Landgren, (We had been quite a few years in America, but we'd never had a special tree to decorate.) Our first such tree with all the trimmings was a great surprise to all of us and most enjoyable. Adorned with the most colorful light collation, it pleased Arthur to know it was appreciated so much. He beamed with delight. (The whole family accepted him like one of the family members.) But that wasn't all—he saw that each member had a gift under the tree.

To my knowledge, I could not remember exchanging gifts on Christmases before, but we did do a lot of baking, which was shared with neighbors and friends. Mother gave Russian baked goodies to his parents. I gave Arthur a pen and pencil set. One would think I gave him a bit of heaven; he was so overjoyed. He grabbed me and kissed me on the cheek. I pulled away as I noticed his mother watching out the corner of her eye. His brother Harry didn't get home for that Christmas vacation; and the home showed he was missing by the emptiness of his corner. He was going to college and decided to stay there and work the summer to have cash for fall tuition. Raya and I stayed awhile and then left for home after wishing them a Merry Christmas.

I'll bet our Christmas tree won the contest for staying up the longest of any Christmas tree—it was up until it shed its former green needles—which had turned to brown ones. One evening when Arthur just happened by he offered to take the decorations and lights off and throw away the tree. It was removed to the wood shed and chopped up for kindling—the last of the tree fragments. Thereafter, a Christmas tree was a gift to mother each year from Arthur. Mother looked forward to this.

COURTING DAYS

Arthur was a patient person with me, until I started working in the theater. He realized there was some competition and his time wasn't his own with me. Every time that he could, he'd be there to pick me up and we'd grab the street car home. A few months later, he surprised me by buying a car which was much nicer than waiting for street cars. This was convenient for him too. Well he got there earlier to protect me, or so he'd say if there were any young men clustered about me as was a particular ticket taker. They would be laughing and teasing, in a nice way. And if Arthur came in and saw that, he'd walk up and say,

"Break it up! You are holding up the line."

They'd look at him and walk into the show room. Arthur would sit way in the back row, so he could watch me. One of the young men walked up and spoke to the ticket taker, so she told him Arthur was my boyfriend. He came back in and whispered to me,

"You are not engaged to him are you?"

I shook my head at him and he walked out of the theater smiling. That was his fourth time seeing the same show. I was too silent on the way home. He knew I didn't approve of his behavior.

"I'm sorry," he said.

This only released my pent up anger. After I got through, he was crushed. Well, I felt sorry too, but I didn't say so at the time.

"I love you so much. I can't bear to have anyone around you, besides everybody does not have good intentions," he said.

This was a new switch for me to hear, as my thoughts never ran in such channels, and I never assumed anyone else's thoughts did either. I still was unhappy about his conduct. He apologized to me again. I accepted his apology. Then he asked me if he could see me that evening.

"No," I said. "I think we have been seeing each other too often. It would be better if we saw less of each other."

"You are really angry, to punish me like that!" he said—pale and hurt.

"Oh, don't feel too badly," I said.

"I just think it will be healthier for both of us and something to look forward too. I like some time to myself. And I'm sure your folks would like to see more of you," I said smiling.

We parted friendly. He promised to call before coming over. Mother wondered why Arthur was not around like he used to be. I told her we had a better understanding as to time.

"Mother, after all it feels good to be able to have free time to myself, and I am sure you enjoy it too."

It turned out to be a very pleasant arrangement for me. What I did not know was that Arthur met the street car each time he was able to and saw that I got home all right, without me knowing.

One night, I became ill at work, so I went home earlier. That was a night of all nights for poor Arthur. He waited until the last streetcar and no Frasinia. My brother Mike had just gotten home from his night out. He was not very quiet.

"Is that you, Mike?"

"Yeah, sorry I woke you up," he said.

"Oh, I was not sleeping too soundly, as I got ill and came home early."

Just then there was a knock on the door. Mike went to open the door and Arthur walked in.

"What's wrong, Arthur?"

"I waited for Frasinia, and she didn't show up. I am worried Mike that something may have happened to her."

"She has been in bed for hours, Arthur."

Arthur rushed past Mike and looked into Raya's and my bedroom.

"How come you were waiting for me?" I said.

"I have done it quite often—without your knowledge?"

"Why, in this cold weather?"

"I can't stand not seeing you."

Then he turned and walked out. Mike must have talked with him before he left for home, because he came into our room.

"Gosh sis, you are rough on that guy. He really loves you!"

I told Mike what he did when I was at work and that I was so ashamed and in danger of losing my job. Mike just looked at me with a concerned look on his face.

"All I can say sis—it looks serious from my point of view. You better think about it."

"Not tonight, brother. I am sick and need rest."

He bid goodnight to both of us gals and went into his bedroom. Arthur called me the next morning before I was to leave for work and asked if he could meet me at the streetcar stop near my home and take me home. As I did not have much time for talk, I said.

"Yes."

It was snowing and cold that evening, as I stepped off the streetcar. He was covered with soft snow, stomping his feet and swinging his arms to keep warm. He took my hand as I was stepping down off the streetcar.

"How long have you been here?" I asked.

"Not too long, but it is cold," he answered.

I noticed he stepped over and picked up a package, as we started towards my home. It was almost 11 p.m. as I had worked until 10 p.m. The house was nice and cozy, as we walked into the kitchen. It was filled with the fragrance of Borscht and homemade bread that mother prepared that day. Borscht was setting on the back of the cooking range. We both had a bowel of Borscht, bread and a glass of milk. We made small talk quietly, as not to awaken anyone. Knowing my mother, I am sure she was still waiting for her last chick to bed down. Arthur didn't stay too late after eating, so before taking leave, he said,

"I have a gift for you that I hope you'll like. It's sort of an apology—please accept it."

I opened it. It was a beautiful brown leather overnight case. It had a brush, comb, soap holder, fingernail buffer and the rest of a manicuring set. Oh, yes—and it also had a toothbrush holder and on the bottom of the case was a five-pound box of chocolate candy.

"This is lovely, but I can't accept this!" I said.

"Oh, please keep it. I just want to taste the candy."

Then we both laughed and had a piece of candy. Good thing we did, as that was the last taste we had. I thought I had put it away in a good place, but the little mice or more ate it all up. I walked into the kitchen one morning with an empty box. Mama looked at me and realized that I had no knowledge of what took place.

"Frasinia, dad and I had some. We had no idea that you knew nothing about it."

I left the empty box on the living room table, to let the others know that I knew who did it, but the only comments I got were

"Well, you didn't offer us any."

I really had forgotten to offer them any, but good heavens—it was only two days since I got the chocolates.

"Just the same, you wait until you are offered next time," I said.

Arthur called up and asked if he could come over.

"Yes," I said.

When he came over he noticed that the box was empty. He laughed and said,

"Here I was going to ask you for a piece of candy. I see there are others with a sweet tooth besides myself."

Thereafter, he'd always see to it that I had a box of candy or chewing gum—too bad, as we had never ever indulged in sweets before. It was considered a special treat and not an eating habit. Not even sweet pastry was served often in our home. Mother had to put a stop to it in a nice way. Arthur respected my mother's wishes. His mother's home was always filled with the fragrance of delicious pastry baking. We did baking too, but more moderately and less sweet. After all mother's children won first prize for having the most perfect teeth in the county, and maybe she was not about to let sweets spoil that. Sweets were replaced with baskets of fruit and nuts. What a man. His mind was working double time. Mother couldn't object to that.

Mother raised a beautiful garden and would see that his mother would have vegetables from it while they were in season. So the web was weaving around my free world. I decided on a much needed vacation. I made plans to visit my sister Olga in Spokane, Washington, and do some thinking, as I had very little chance at home. I told mother of my plans and why.

"What are you going to tell Arthur?" she asked.

"Just what I am telling you."

I took time off from my work and left. My sister Olga was happy to see me as it had been years since we saw each other. I wasn't there very long before my mother came to take me home. She was concerned about me and what was taking place at home. It seemed that Arthur's mother came over and begged her to go and get me, as her son told her he had so desire to live without me.

"Frasinia, I don't think you can take this lightly."

"Mother, I am not! I just don't want to get married yet."

"All right!" she said, "Just don't let anything happen that you may be sorry for—for the rest of your life."

"What can happen mother?" I don't believe that he'll harm himself."

"Oh yes, people have done so dear, many times. Why don't you come home and have a talk with him. I am sure he will be reasonable and wait until you are ready. Don't you care for him?"

"I am very fond of him mother, but I can't say that my feelings are the same as his."

"I don't think that you'll ever feel like he does, dear. Sometimes love comes after marriage," mother said.

"Isn't that rather taking a chance even for him?" I replied.

"Well, we'll see, dear."

She only stayed a couple of days and then we packed up and left for home. Mother's face looked sad; she was not the kind to hide her feelings when it concerned others. I was not too happy myself. When we arrived home, it was quite late. Dad and Mike met us. Not much was said after the greeting. Dad remarked that I caused quite a commotion, which could have been avoided, if only I had come to mother and him and talked over my feelings—although I did mention to mother before I left that I needed a vacation from the pressure that was put on me by Arthur and had to have time to think. Guess it was not enough.

We all retired for the might. Mike winked as he said goodnight. The following evening Arthur came over. My folks, Arthur, and I had a long talk. Arthur agreed to be more patient. He said he was sorry he made me feel that way, so that I felt I had to get away. Father even suggested that it might be advisable for us to have other dates. I knew this did not set too well with Arthur, but he did not disagree.

"I have no intention of dating others; it's up to Frasinia if that is her desire," Arthur said as he looked at me with sad filled eyes.

"It's getting late. I better go home."

He got up and started walking to the front door. He curtsied to my parents and bid the rest of us goodnight and left. I heard my father say to mother,

"Too bad Frasinia doesn't realize that such love is offered only once in a lifetime."

There were other men that wanted to date me, but somehow, I didn't seem too anxious to go out with them. When Arthur and I would go out dancing, I'd dance with them, but I guess God blessed Arthur with his patience.

As time went on I began to look forward to his visits. I felt so safe and content with him, so when he asked if I'd become engaged to him on my 19th birthday, I agreed. The following June 15, 1929 we were married in church with a few friends and family. After the ceremony, we came home to the reception. Shortly after that, Arthur went home to get into his going away apparel, and I into mine, slacks, boots and sport shirt.

Arthur had the car ready and packed with camping equipment and groceries to last for a couple weeks. We had planned to spend our honeymoon camping in Glacier Park, Montana. We were to drive as far as my brother Nick's place that afternoon.

My niece Olga Letz came along to help my sister-in-law to take care at her twin baby sons, while they did the harvesting. When we got there, it was quite late and we found no one at home. It had been raining all the while, since we left home. Rain was supposed to represent a special omen—blessed with good luck. It did not start out that way. Arthur depended on me to show him the way. Well—I thought I remembered well, but to this day, I'll invariably get people lost. With a lot of inquiring, we finally arrived to an empty and dark house, and it was very late. I was waiting for Arthur to get out of the car, and when he didn't I looked up at him as he said,

"I'm so sorry; you'll have to help me."

Olga and I got out of the car; we walked to the house and tried the door; then thinking that maybe they left the door open for us, I searched for the key in the most remote places—no such luck. Then I tried the window and it raised up, so I called Olga to find me a stick to prop it up with. Then I crawled through the window to try opening the door from the inside—but I couldn't. I crawled back out through the window. I helped Arthur out of the car—and he leaned on my shoulder.

"I don't think you are strong enough, Frasinia. I should have a long stick to hold me up."

I don't know where my strength came from, but with God's help, we managed to help him through the window. I called to Olga to have a chair handy for him to grab onto when he got inside the house. He sat down on the chair. I followed after him, and I noticed that he was very pale, with increasing pain on his face.

"What's the matter?" and "Why didn't you say something before?" I asked him.

He looked at me with tears in his eyes. He finally told me that this had happened to him before, but not as severe—it was his heart. I was shocked with the thought, that I could lose him, realizing how dear he had become to me. I quietly fixed up the sofa bed and helped him onto it. Ten year old Olga stood by helplessly with tears in her eyes. When I got Arthur settled, I took her by the hand and walked with her into the kitchen—as we had not eaten since leaving my home, at noon, and it was now 10 p.m.

All we could do was to wait for Nick and his family to come home, since they had no phone and farmers were far and few in between. Arthur seemed to be breathing with less pain and more comfort. I went out and brought food from the car and a sleeping bag for Olga. After a warm meal, we all felt better. With the range fire going the chill was taken out of the house. We washed up the dishes and tidied up the kitchen.

I spread the sleeping bag on the floor in the living room close to the sofa bed to help give Olga more comfort from her traumatic experience. Turning down the coal-oil lamp, I was just getting ready to bed down by my niece, so as not to disturb Arthur. Just then he opened his eyes and asked me to lie down beside him.

"I was afraid, to cause your pain to return if I should move," I said.

"My pain would be greater without you in my arms," he smiled sadly.

I lay down beside him quietly and soon the house, too, was quiet. We could hear the rain had started up again. It seemed for only a short time that we had fallen asleep when my brother Nick and his family returned. It was 3 a.m.

"We were wondering why the light was on in the house, since the house was locked," Nick said.

Nearing their place, they had recognized our car. After our

explanation as to how we got in and what took place, it was a second shock to them. Their neighbor had had a heart attack and they had to take him to the doctor and then decided to stay with the children until the neighbor's wife returned from the hospital. We didn't spend too much time talking as it was late, so they went to bed.

The next morning, Arthur was still feeling badly, so Nick drove up to his neighbor who had a phone and called the doctor. He drove up that afternoon from Conrad, Montana. In the meantime, Julia (Nick's wife) had Arthur moved into their bedroom, which was more private and with a comfortable bed. By moving him, his pain returned and he became delirious—which frightened me. When the doctor arrived he gave him some medication to quiet him down and kill the pain. The doctor stayed around for a few hours. He gave me instructions and said he'd be back the next day, unless he was needed sooner and not to hesitate calling anytime.

The evening brought more fever. I was up all night with him. He called for his mother to cut up his legs and cook them. I was crying softly, so as not to disturb the others, but they got up and asked if they could be of any help. I went out to the car and brought in my towels and dish towels—warmed them up and wrapped up his legs and arms and covered him up more to stop his shaking. Soon he fell asleep and broke out with perspiration. The fever broke and he slept more soundly. The next day the doctor came in the morning and checked him over. He told me I did the right thing, as we kept him from going into pneumonia. He started to feel better as time went on.

Our honeymoon was spent at Nick's place. Arthur felt badly to have me as his nurse instead of his wife. I was only too happy to have him get well. At least that was a blessing from God. The doctor's last visit informed me that Arthur was strong enough to travel back to Great Falls, Montana.

Our trip home was quite uneventful; he slept most of the time. I drove the car home, and I did not get lost; it was daylight. My thoughts were many, as to what reaction would his folks have; what would they say to me.

When I drove up to the house, his brother Harry ran down the front steps and kissed me.

"I am collecting the kiss, even if it is late."

"Harry, Arthur had a heart attack; he was very sick," I said.

He looked at me and realized that I had no knowledge of Arthur's past history of rheumatic fever.

"The folks were concerned that might happen," he said.

I must have been all eyes as I looked at him. He turned quickly to help Arthur out of the car. Arthur's father came out and between the two of them, they carried him upstairs to one of the bedrooms. I heard Harry calling the family doctor. In a short time the doctor came up and examined Arthur; then he turned and looked at me and said,

"You just about became a widow the day of your marriage. He is very fortunate to have office work. And with your care he'll be all right, but he must stay in bed at least a month," the doctor said.

Nothing seemed to register to me, as I watched their facial expressions. All of a sudden, I felt tired and sad; Harry noticed and said,

"Frasinia is tired and perhaps hungry, too."

After the doctor left, I walked up to Arthur in his bed,

"I hope you don't mind if I go up to see my folks for awhile; you'll have plenty of care here. I am sure they are concerned about us."

"You should, I'll be all right."

I told his folks where I was going and that I'd be back shortly.

"Aren't you going to have something to eat first?

"I'm really not hungry, thank you," I said as I walked out the front door.

My folks noticed our return and Arthur being helped into the house—they were all questions. I explained to them all that I knew and understood myself. They were so sorry to hear that Arthur had a heart attack; they were very fond of him.

After a month of rest Arthur started getting around again. In another month he started back to work. Even with office work he'd come home exhausted, though he never complained. He accepted his condition, and we soon adjusted to life and found days of happiness with all the drawbacks.

Shortly after that we moved into a rental my brother Mike had in Burlingame, a suburb of Black Eagle, Montana. It had three rooms, but it was far from being modern in all respects—water and lights— yes, but there was a little house back of the big house at the far end of the lot—and it was pretty cold when the north wind blew the snow about. Since I had known days like these in the years past, I was not unhappy about it. The adjustment was quickly taken in stride. We made the place quite comfortable and homey.

We raised a lovely garden, which was needed very much, as The Depression was strangling the countryside. Our table was never empty of food, not only for us, but by those that made a habit of dropping in just about meal time. Many times we'd have a two course meal and still felt so blessed. Many of our friends were without work— some that had homes were indebted to the grocery stores for food. They found it hard to buy them back when they finally found part time work and some were hired back to their former jobs. Oh yes, my thirty customers for free haircuts went down to zero as soon as they got jobs, which was fine with me, for I had to make plans for something more exciting in my life than sweeping up locks of hair.

Mother was missing the two youngest sons at meal times almost every day. Maurice and George would come over a little before, so naturally we'd ask them to share our food. Arthur would ask them if they were keeping me company while he was at work. Yes that—and they liked my cooking, which I had changed to please my husband.

"Gosh boys—and here I like your mother's cooking," Arthur said laughing.

Mother and I had a heart to heart talk on these missing sons and they soon became once a week guests.

Shortly after my marriage sister Olga wrote to mama asking if Raya could come and live with her. Mother thought it would be a nice change for Raya as we were very close and my marriage seemed to have made Raya lonely. This made the Letz's home seem emptier to George. Maurice and Bill found many things to do, as their work was cut out for them daily at home or in the fields. I missed Raya very much myself, but as time went by, adjustment to my new life took place. If I had nothing to do—I made work for myself. The place was kept washed so much that a new coat of paint had to be redone in six months of our residency. Of course as time went on, I found other interests to take place besides a pan of hot suds.

George's concerns about my coming home were real to him. It was about 9:30 p.m. when I received a phone call from him. He was alone at home which was most unusual in mother's house.

"Where are mother and dad?" I asked.

"They are visiting their Russian friends in Sand Coulee" (a small town east of Great Falls, Montana—about 25 miles from home.).

"Where are Maurice and Bill?"

"Out! They said they'd be right back, but it's late and I am afraid to be alone. Why don't you come home? You have been away too long already."

"George, I am married now and must live with my husband. Since its night and we are both alone at our homes, why don't you lock the doors there, as I have here? Just say a prayer and I am sure you'll be fine."

"Oh, all right—goodnight."

"Let me know tomorrow how everything was—all right George?"

Next morning, he ran over to see me. We talked quietly in the kitchen as Arthur was sleeping. We came to a better understanding of why I wasn't living at home.

OUR FIRST CHILD

After two years our daughter Marlene was born November 25, 1931. We were proud parents of a beautiful baby with auburn hair and blue eyes. At five months, she took ill—one of her lung lobes collapsed. She was given from 48 to 72 hours to live. The doctors could not figure out what caused it as there was no sign of infection in her body. Our family doctor called in other doctors to study her case. Even doctors out of state were talked with and they were puzzled, as her X-rays didn't show anything but a deflated lobe.

We came to the hospital to see our little daughter only to hear such heart breaking news. The doctors would only let one of us go in at a time. Arthur went in first. When the doctor and Arthur left, I sat down and lost myself in conversation with God. I don't know how long the doctor stood there watching me. I felt someone shaking me gently, calling my name. I realized it was the doctor looking down at me smiling and he said,

"I have been trying to tell you that something took place while we were in the baby's room. I am sure your baby is going to live. Her breathing is normal and her color came back. It is a good sign! It seems like a miracle."

My heart was so full of gratitude to God, that all I could say was

"Thank you—Thank you," and I walked hastily into her room.

Arthur was holding her little hands with the most loving look on his face. The baby was smiling at him. I stepped close by him and just watched. After our gratitude and thank you prayers to God, we left for home, with a promise that tomorrow we'd be able to take Marlene home.

It was a lovely spring day in April when we brought our baby home. As days and months went by she grew stronger and healthier. The doctors were pleased with her recovery, but our prayers to God continued each day—thanking him for his miracle.

RENTING MY FOLKS' HOME

One bright morning my father walked over to see us and asked if we would like to move into one, of his houses, which was more modern and larger—just for the payments that he was making on it. Well, that was a bargain—$19 a month. My brother had no problem renting the house we were living in. We were happy to move and did so in a short time. It had a closed in yard with a big garden space. Marlene was just crawling about at the time we moved in; a closed in yard was a blessing.

The Great Depression was still in full swing. Jobs were hard to come by, even the proud were begging for food. Our garden was a blessing not only for us, but for other hungry souls. I got so I felt guilty if there was chicken on our table and we did not call someone to share it with us.

We did not own a car at that time. We couldn't afford one; so we were called the walking family. Our big concern was food, a roof over our head, and clothes on our back. Still we were blessed to share with the less fortunate.

I recall one of my many sharing times. This particular day as I was in the garden gathering vegetables for my evening meal, a young man came to the back gate and asked if there was something he could do for some food. As I was anxious to have them on their way, I picked a bunch of assorted vegetables and gave them to him. He thanked me very much and left. No sooner had he left and another one came up and walked into the yard rather boldly.

"Boy, you sure have a wonderful garden. If I had some of those vegetables I'd make a stew."

I picked another bunch and gave to him. Picking up my pan, I walked quietly into the house, and just as I was going to hook the screen door, he stuck his foot into the door way.

"If I had some meat, it would taste better," he said.

"So would ours," I answered. "Now please get your foot out."

I spoke loudly—hoping someone would hear. Heaven bless my brother Nick. He was back of the garage unbeknownst to me.

"What in the hell is going on here?" Nick questioned loudly.

He had a wrench in his hand as he walked rapidly towards the door.

"I just wanted to thank her," the stranger said.

"Well you have. Now beat it and don't come back here again!" Nick shouted.

Boy—did the stranger move fast. Nick warned me about opening doors to any that was a stranger at any time—my lesson for the day—there were different kinds of hunger. Strange, but there were not many coming to our place after that—the message must have been forwarded to others, besides my door was always locked when I was alone.

There was an empty lot, next to the folks' home, and the folks owned it also. Mother put in a garden on the lot, besides the one in their back yard. Between the three gardens, we had plenty to can. It was a good feeling when canning was over and such a pleasure to see rows upon rows of loving labor well spent.

Autumn was another beautiful season of the year. When one has more time to go fishing, hiking, picnicking or just visiting with friends—one of the many of God's beautiful gifts.

School was in full swing at this time, but weekends were always your own. Our vacations were spent camping out in the mountains by a stream, when we had a car. One could adjust to meet any circumstance if taken in stride.

After living in this place for two years, dad asked us if we'd like to buy it. But our budget was so poor that we couldn't do it. Dad had a chance to sell it, to a young couple that got married, for some gain, so he did. Arthur's parents asked us to move into their small house in back of the lot. How could we refuse five dollars a month? Of course it needed repairs and painting which we were glad to do.

Arthur's parents had a beautiful six bedroom two-story home with a full basement on a corner lot—beautifully landscaped, so the small house in the back had a lovely setting. Since Arthur worked two weeks a month, we had a hard time to make ends meet. This was another blessing for us. It had three rooms, clothes closet, and a cellar. The commode and wash bowl were put into the clothes closet.

With all the nice friends we had—to help, it didn't take long before the house was finished inside and out. The only thing missing was a bathtub—a galvanized wash tub was used to bath in.

"Why don't you come and use our bathroom. I am sure it's less trouble and more convenient," I heard dad Landgren say to Arthur one day.

"Gosh—it's about time you took a bath."

"I suppose it is dad," Arthur said smiling.

He told him how we bathed. Regardless which tub we used, we kept clean.

One afternoon dad Landgren came over and asked if I'd come over and take care of mother Landgren as he had to go to work. Mother got a severe gallstone attack that morning. The doctor had been over and gave her a shot to kill the pain and left. I took the baby and went over, leaving a note for Arthur.

Mother was asleep. I started to prepare a meal for the family in their home, as they had two boarders living there. This went on for two weeks. I had to spend the nights with mother, and Arthur and Marlene spent the nights at home. Since Arthur worked days, I'd get up early and get the baby ready to have with me and he'd eat breakfast with the men and leave for work. Dad Landgren would come just in time to have breakfast and visit with mother and go to bed. He had worked the afternoon shift for years.

Dad Landgren's hobby was repairing clocks, which could have

been very profitable if his heart was not so big. He was a king man to his fellow man, never refused to help if it was possible. He had clocks hanging on walls and setting around in his room that he used for sort of a workshop. You could just imagine trying to sleep when the clocks started giving out their own sound of chimes. The first few nights were like a nightmare—until I learned to shut out the chimes, or maybe I was just was too tired to listen anymore.

I washed clothes a few times while I was there. Mother had spoiled these men. She pressed their stockings and underclothes. Well—I wasn't in the habit of doing that, since we never did it at home. Dad was surprised when I had his underclothes just folded and stockings rolled in pairs—all laying on his bed. The others did not make any comments.

"Frasinia, they are not pressed," dad said.

"Yes, that is right, dad. I never did it at home and I can't see why it should be done around here either."

"Mother always does it," he said.

"You men better start taking care of her more; she has a ten room house and two boarders besides entertaining friends. It is just too much."

The two boarders were taking this conversation in, and mother heard too, as she called from her bedroom,

"Papa, come here."

When he came back to eat his dinner, he just sat down and didn't say another word. I was happy when mother got well. I am sure dad was too, as things went back to normal for him.

Our second child was born—a little girl. One of the valves didn't close at birth, so we lost her at five months.

The Great Depression was not just crawling, but running from all corners of our dear Country. My darling daughter Marlene (4 years old) would swing on the gate, and if anyone walked by, she'd say,

"Are you hungry? My mama will give you a sandwich."

These two men looked like they just jumped out of the boxcar. I lifted her off the gate and led her into the house and locked the door. I heard their laugher as they walked on. I sat my child down and tried to explain why she shouldn't do that again.

"But mama, you do feed lots of people."

"Yes, honey, but you must not call anyone's attention to it, because we don't want to get hurt by some of them, besides we may not have any food left for ourselves."

Since Arthur's take home pay was only $68 a month, we were lucky that one of our parents raised a garden. The place we were living at now had no space for a garden. It was beautifully landscaped with borders of beautiful flowers, trees, and the rest was in grass— even their inside porches were filled with houseplants. Dad Landgren enjoyed taking care of them, and mother worked at it too.

My mother is the one in our family who loved to work with the vegetables and flowers. Her yard was like a jungle filled with vast varieties of them. The vegetable garden supplied not only for people but there was enough for the bugs. Nothing was sprayed in the yard except the potatoes which were sprinkled with water. If that did not work, they were hand picked and burned in coal oil. We helped mother with her garden and canning; that way we had use of it too.

SAVING DIMES

Our only savings at that time was putting small coins into a Log Cabin syrup can. It was surprising how it grew, even dimes at that time. After a year we had saved $160. Arthur asked me what was my pleasure—a trip, buy clothes, or what.

"No—I want to buy a home of our own!"

"But Frasinia, this isn't enough to buy a home!"

"Then we'll save some more."

By now we had a secondhand car, so we could drive around and see if we could find an old building for sale out in the country. I thought Arthur had told his father what I said. I guess they decided to pacify me. In the meantime, my father decided to sell the lot mother raised her garden in. He asked us if we would be interested in buying it. We were, and we did. This was a start—fifty dollars less in our piggy bank, but back to saving again—more dimes. Arthur found me counting dimes one day and asked how much we had.

"It will take a few more years of saving," he said.

"Oh, no, friends of ours went out into the country and found an old building for $100—had it brought in and now they are fixing it into a nice home."

He looked at me and smiled, shaking his head. The Depression caused many people to give up their homes, or to sell them for just enough to take them to their relatives, or someplace else that might help them find a job. It would not be uncommon to find a place for sale at a price even we could afford.

Many of our Sundays were spent driving around the countryside looking for a building. Early one Sunday morning, we took off with dad and mother Landgren to see if we would have better luck that day. I always carried the piggy bank with me on such times when we were looking. Low and behold—a country schoolhouse for sale. We stopped to inspect it. The schoolhouse was 30 by 30 feet with a teacherage built to it. At that time a teacher lived in by the school, especially if the school was far out of the way. It had a wide hallway the length of the schoolhouse, a high ceiling and the floor was in good condition—for only $130, the asking price. A notice was nailed to a door where we could get in touch with the party that took care at it. So we drove up to the farmer's place. Arthur and dad told me it would cost too much to have it moved onto the lot.

"I understand, but we can do it," I said.

They couldn't talk me out of it. The farmer agreed to watch it for a couple months or until we arranged for the movers. Arthur gave in to my reasoning. Mother and dad Landgren were rather reluctant as times were very unsure yet. We counted out $125 in dimes to the farmer and received a receipt. With only $20 left, we were back to saving again.

There was much discussion on the way home how and with what to move the building. It was 30 miles to where our lot was. Dad moved things before and knew what processes one had to take. I listened to their conversation, but nothing drowned out my dreams.

"Oh, my father had Mr. Weeds help him move," I said. "Why don't we get in touch with him before we worry too much? Then we'll know the price and what can be done."

"Fine, we'll do just that," Arthur said.

As we drove into the yard, dad asked if we'd come in and have dinner with them and play cards. (It was one of his most enjoyable pastimes.) If it was possible, we never refused our parents' wishes, so we said yes. While I helped mother prepare dinner, the moving discussion was in full swing again. After dinner and the dishes were taken care of, the card game started and lasted to 12 p.m. It would have lasted longer but Arthur had to go to work early the next morning.

Mr. Weeds lived in Conrad, Montana, so I wrote him a letter; his wife must have gotten the message as he called us a few days later. He said that since he had a lot of moving to do for a party in Great Falls, Montana, the price would be reasonable for us. After our explanation to him, that he'd have plenty of help, the size of the school building with the teacherage, and the distance the buildings would have to be moved, he decided that he'd have one of his smaller moving rigs do the job. The best part was that after we got the basement dug and foundation poured—he'd come back and place the building down on the foundation and do it all for $150; that is if we would have the work done before October as he had other work through the month before going home. Since it was still May, time was on our side—Glory be!

Arthur checked with the lumber company for materials to do the basement. Yes, they would give us credit. He borrowed $150 against his life insurance to move the buildings. We had the schoolhouse and teacherage moved before the month was up. My brother Maurice was living with our parents next door to us. He made a bid on digging the basement for $100 and hired a few men for $2 an hour to help him. Poor fellow—he had no idea that the lot had a mass of rocks to dig out.

We had a standing audience watching the schoolhouse take form to become our home. (The teacherage was placed to the rear of the lot and later sold to my brother Matt and moved to his place.) Finally our home was ready to move into and we spent our first Christmas in it. It was not a complete Christmas as we lost dad Landgren from a heart attack just a short while before that. His birthday was on Christmas Eve. Christmas Eve did not seem right without celebrating dad Landgren's birthday and opening a package.

Since winter had arrived, not much more could be done, so we'd have to wait until better days. Marlene was in first grade and going to school with her cousin Phyllis who was five months older, but they were taken for twins at times. They sat side by side in school, but that was not the best idea. Finally the teacher took care of that. Their friendship, devotion, and concern for each other prospered throughout childhood and that connection has continued to this day.

Another Christmas was upon us but with a lot of snow this time that would stay for awhile. So much joyful camaraderie from the snow and Christmas, but the year was very lean, as we were still paying for the house which was the biggest gift of all. There were gifts for the folks and the children under the tree. As usual we celebrated on Christmas Eve; dad Landgren was missed by all, and our hearts were filled with sadness for a father who was a kind and good man.

After dinner was over and the packages were opened, Phyllis and Marlene went to bed. I heard some crying coming from the bedroom. I went to check.

"What's the matter? Didn't you like your presents?"

"Yes—we do, but if we'd have a baby brother, or a sister, we'd be happier," they said.

"What brought this on?"

Well, it seemed their friend Dorothy had a baby brother and they didn't.

"Why don't you two say your prayers and go to sleep?" I asked.

So it was agreed. We heard them ask in their prayer for such a gift for next Christmas. The girls were smiling when I returned to the group.

Marlene's prayers were answered on October 14, 1939—her baby brother was born. Phyllis' baby sister was born. However, Arthur's health was failing; the doctors told him to take it easy. It was not that easy trying to hold down a job to take care of his responsibilities and still find time to rest, but where there is a will there is a way.

I DARED GOD

In 1946, I dared god to take my loved ones from me, if he loved them more than I. I think of it often—how I could have gambled with someone else's life at stake. This daring all started from the very first day of my marriage. My husband took sick on the day of our wedding; how he went through the vows with such pain, I still can't figure out.

When we went on our honeymoon, I still had no knowledge of his illness until he had to get out of the car and couldn't move without my help. The place we stopped for that evening was my brother's and then to add to my great shock, I found no one was home. I opened the window and pushed Arthur, my husband, through the window. When I finally got him to bed, he was out of his mind with pain. We stayed there for a week.

The following morning my brother and his wife came home. They'd had to leave on an emergency to a neighbor's farm and had to spend the night with the children there while the man took his wife to the hospital. When my brother Nick came home, he went to get the doctor immediately. After the doctor's examination, he said that Arthur had Inflammatory Rheumatism, and it had done damage all ready to his heart. I nearly became a widow the first day of my marriage.

The medicine the doctor left relieved Arthur enough to let us travel back home. I drove the car back and Arthur slept. He needed sleep; this was the first sleep he had had in the whole week. When we arrived home, his folks didn't seem badly hurt. They told me later that this had happened before during his boyhood days.

Now came days of nursing him back to health as well as I could with that sickness he had acquired. After a few months, our life started to look better—almost as any other young married couple. Arthur went to work in an office. It was a good thing that he could work in one. The doctor said that his labor days were over.

After Arthur went to work, we were able to move and live by ourselves. But just as we moved, I had to get sick and this put us back with his folks again. Finally by Christmas we were again able to move back by ourselves. Two years went by, and we found out that we were to have a little gift from heaven. I was going to have a baby. That November a baby girl came to stay. We thought that she was the prettiest baby in the world, but that was the privilege of the parents to feel that way about their own. It seemed, however, that our happiness was short-lived.

Our baby took ill. The doctors said that she would not live more than 48 to 72 hours. Her left lung had collapsed and they couldn't figure out how it happened. Arthur and I were brokenhearted, of all things—why did God want our baby? The baby had not even been baptized. We decided to attend to that right away. That same evening she was baptized in the hospital room—then came hours of waiting. The hours seemed to fly. I had resigned myself, after daring God to take her if he loved her more than I did. I was sitting in the sun parlor when the doctor came into the room. I expected the worst, but he told me that our baby would live. His voice seemed far away; he had to repeat it again and again. I went into the baby's room. There was Arthur holding her in his arms with a happiness that I had never seen on his face before. My heart knew no greater happiness either. The life of our little girl was spared! We were able to take our baby home the next day. No one knew how she recovered so quickly but she was well again and that was all that mattered.

Almost four years had passed and another baby girl was born, but she was born a blue baby. At five months she died. About three years later, we decided to make a home of our own. We had just finished it enough to move into it comfortably when I found out that I was to have another baby. While building a home, Arthur started to be bothered with a pain in his chest. He went through an examination, which proved beyond a shadow of a doubt—he had heart trouble.

The day I came home with our first son we thought as before that we would have complete happiness, but there was a shadow hanging over us because of Arthur's condition. All in all, life was sweet; we were so grateful for moments that came through darkness—moments that were bright and sunny. Our son was doing wonderfully—growing fast and feeling well. When he was sixteen months old, there was an epidemic of strep throat going around. He had to get it, even with my careful care. He was soon taken to the hospital. He was made as comfortable as possible, but I still knew that the specialists had given him up. His ears were affected by the strep throat. All the doctors could do was to wait until his throat cleared up. After three weeks the baby had a double mastoid operation, but it was too late—the condition turned chronic. I wasn't any good staying home so I stayed at the hospital with him. They said that he would have a rigid back or some ill effect, but it did not leave anything. When I heard this, I felt as if life was flowing out of me. I prayed for God to save him, but if he left him with a crippled body or mind, to take him.

A change soon came over the baby. He seemed to relax and really rest. He moved normally without moaning. The next day he stood up in his crib. Everybody was amazed. The baby recovered after two months of nursing. We brought him home but as I said before it left his ears in a chronic condition, and they still were after seven years of doctor's care. But it didn't seem to stunt his growth. The last report from the doctor said that he might be that way for the rest of his life, or he might grow out of it. We still had hopes.

We had been married for 18 years and it seemed to me one of the beds was always holding one or the other member of the family. Through all the dark days and trials, we had days of happiness. There seemed to be an end to everything, so we just couldn't lie down and end it—we had to wait our time.

Although no knows how tired I was at times. I tried to keep happiness at my home—to keep spirits up even if they were just my own. As I helped my children say their evening prayer, I tried to add all the things that I wanted my little family to have for their own well being. At the end of their prayer, I'd always say, under my breath,

"And, dear Father—give me courage, strength, and faith for the days that are yet to come. Amen"

A SON BORN

October 14, 1939 was a joyful day for us, as our son came into our lives. We were informed by the doctor that he was a healthy baby, which would be wonderful news for any parent to hear.

Those days one was kept in the hospital for two weeks. Time seemed to go by so slowly, as I was anxious to go home and see my little daughter Marlene. She was staying with Judith and Harry Landgren, our dear brother and his wife. She could not have been in better hands, besides she had the company of her cousin Phyllis, almost the same age—just a few weeks apart, but I missed her very much.

When we brought our son home, we hid him behind a pillow on the bed. Marlene ran into the house and came into the bedroom to see her baby brother. After our first greeting, she asked if we had left him at the hospital.

"No—you'll have to find him," Arthur said.

Then the baby made a noise and of course hide-n-seek was over.

Before too long, most of the family paid their respectful visit to see Milton Dale Landgren. Arthur named the daughters that we had and I was to name the sons. I was reading the book called *Man of the Forest* before his birth. I liked the kind gentle man who was the main character in the story, so my many choices came to an end.

Milton was growing beautifully and doing so well. My father would come in and look at him. It seemed he was always sleeping when dad came to see him.

"Daughter, are you sure he is all right—he is sleeping too much."

"Oh, dad, I just cleaned and fed him, although he does seem

sleepy; even when I am washing up and feeding him, he just gives me a sleepy smile and baby noises."

But after four months, he became wide awake to see what this world was all about. He still slept a lot, but it pleased dad to be able to pick him up and hold him awhile, as dad loved children. Both of my parents loved children. All I can say is—there should be more people like my parents.

On January 25, 1940, Judith Landgren had her baby girl, named Barbara. Marlene and Phyllis' prayers were answered. The happy little girls went hand-in-hand, skipping down the street telling the news to their friends. Everything was going along just fine, until an epidemic of streptococcus raged through the states. So many people lost their lives and others were left with chronic conditions.

Barbara was the first one to get streptococcus and then our son at the age of sixteen months old; the illness settled in his ears. What a nightmare! After being in the hospital for three weeks, the doctors decided to operate on his ears as he had mastoiditis. After the operation was performed, what a sick baby—he was between life and death. After two months of hospital care, the baby was still struggling for his life. The only way he was fed was with an eyedropper.

I heard the doctor tell the nurse on his rounds one morning that he did not expect the child to last through the night. I am sure it was not meant for my ears, but I did hear which made me turn to the only great Healer the world has ever known. I bowed my head and dared God, of all things, to take my son if he loved him more than I did. I asked God to leave my son normal in every way, or to take him. I was so deeply involved in talking to God—that it took my son's voice to bring me back. After two months of moaning and weak crying, he had pulled himself up, holding onto the side of the crib—calling out for food.

It was lunch time and food was brought to the patients. The nurse was so astonished that she left quickly and finally came back with some food. She placed it in the crib; he sat down beside it and ate every bit of it. I lifted him in my arms and held him gently.

"Oh, thank you God for the great miracle!"

When the doctor and the nurse made the evening rounds, they were amazed at his recovery.

"I don't understand," said the doctor.

I told him that I heard what he said to the nurse, so I turned to God for help and his great love performed a miracle. The nurse said rather angrily,

"We never get credit."

"You must remember, there is a greater Healer than we are," the doctor said to her.

The doctor told me that he seemed to be on the road to recovery, but his ears were still draining. A week later, we brought him home. The first place he walked was to the drawer where I kept bread and helped himself to a slice of bread and ate it all.

Life wasn't that simple and the sun didn't shine every day. But somehow days and years went by. When my son was seven years old and Marlene was fourteen years old, Arthur had another heart attack which put him to bed for seven years. Marlene was in the first year of high school and Milton was in second grade. I was grateful to be able to stay home the first year so I could help all to adjust to a new set of rules—mostly for the children. The second year, I went to work half days and Marlene a few hours after school and on Saturdays. Judith would check Arthur a couple times before I'd come home.

After I started to work full time, I made different arrangements. I prepared a warm lunch for him and put it in the thermos bottle and a sandwich. Judith would still check on him or call me to see if he needed anything. Milton would be home from school at 4 p.m. He would take care of his father's needs until Marlene and I came home. Arthur was allowed to go to the bathroom so that helped out a lot. We had many friends and relatives who would stop in and see him whenever they could. Bless them, as they brought him some outside life to brighten his day.

As my mother was living next door to me, I asked her to come and live with us so I could be of more help to her.

"Heaven forbid!" she'd say, "that I should live with any of you. If you should come and find me dead, well—I am sure you'll know what to do."

For a while, Marlene spent nights with mother, but she became ill. The doctor forbade me to let Marlene do it any longer. So I got one of the neighbor ladies to do it, which lasted two weeks. I finally had to set the alarm clock a couple times through the night to help mother to the bathroom and back to bed.

Dad had passed away a few years before. This gave mother many hours to reminisce the past. Mother took advantage of such luxuriousness and was so wise to do so. It was often that one could find her weeping quietly and at the same time looking beautiful. The reflection on her face would express delight, pain, and love, as past and present paraded through her thoughts.

My heart cried out in anguish for mother before I learned that it was her outlet of relief from her built up emotion. I'd put my arms around her and ask,

"Mother, what's the matter?"

"Dear, you should do it; it helps so much for your soul," she said.

Reflecting later I thought—how true. I should have listened, but at the time I'd always answer,

"Mother, I have not the time for such luxury, besides it always invites questions to be answered and I am sure it is not good for my family."

"Well, dear—you can do it here in my home."

"Yes—I know, but the tattletale eyes and red nose would need to be explained."

"Oh," and then she said with a deep sigh, "perhaps you know better."

Unbeknownst to my mother and to solve her sure unhappiness,

my heart called out silently to God to give me more faith and strength to carry on.

My oldest sister decided to sell out in Florida and come to care for mother. Since her husband was retired, it didn't matter where they lived—so they said. I was happy for mother; she'd have one of her loved ones around all the time. After Eda and Jack came, things seemed to be more enjoyable for mother. As for me, it gave me time to relax a bit myself with the family.

Marlene met a young man on her sixteenth birthday which blossomed into love and marriage. Such a devoted person and companion—he was always ready and willing to help when there was a need.

Arthur lived long enough to see our daughter get married, September 22, 1951. They had a large church wedding; her uncle Harry Landgren walked her down the aisle. The reception was held in a large restaurant; they opened up their double dining area for the occasion. It was a beautiful wedding with five hundred well wishers attending—relatives and friends. I only wished that Arthur was able to attend it and enjoy the beauty of it all. How many friends we had and relatives that came to give their best wishes to our darling daughter and our son-in-law John Warren Willey.

After the reception they drove home and had some pictures taken with her father and my mother as she too was not able to come to the wedding because of her health. Then they left on their honeymoon for the weekend to Helena, Montana, as John had to be back on Monday for work.

They came back to live in an apartment in their Uncle Harry's home. He had a few apartments in his large home. Lucky young couple, but not for long as John was called into the Armed Services before many weeks went by. When John left for his training, Marlene came back home to stay. She had her job to keep her busy through the day.

My Brother Jim's wife had been ailing for over a year. On October

12, 1951 she passed away. Arthur passed away October 13, 1951, in the afternoon. The thing I had dreaded the most happened. My son was with him when it took place. My daughter and I were at work. My brother Nick and his wife were in town visiting with mother next door. Milton ran over to tell them. They called the Doctor and then drove over to pick me up. When we got home, I found the doctor trying to console my son, as he thought he brought it. It was a traumatic experience for a twelve year old boy. It took a long time for him to overcome that vision of death.

Jim came to live with us shortly after we had a double funeral for our loved ones. It was hard for him to adjust to having a child around the place. They never had children of their own.

In the meantime, Eda had been encouraging me to go away to California for awhile. I rented the house to Jim and left for Los Angeles, California, with Milton. My brother George and Sister Raya lived there with their families. By this time Marlene and John were living in San Diego, California. He was through with the training and going to mechanical school while in the service. I got a job at the Al Captain Theater and worked part time on the Dinah Shore Chevy Show. It was very interesting work.

I rented an apartment within walking distance of my work, as school would require busing. Milton begged to go to Academy school. He'd heard so much about what fun it was; well, I thought at least I'd know where he was after school hours when I was working, and besides he'd be home on weekends. Milton and I took the bus to the Academy on Saturday and arranged monthly tuition. They took us to the room where he'd stay with about twenty other young boys. It looked like an open barn to me.

"Is this where the boys sleep?" I asked.

"Oh no, it's temporary until the other quarters are finished."

"And when will that be? My son has ear problems and this would cause him pain."

"We have a nurse and doctor who watch over the children." he said.

178

In my mind I was not happy about the arrangement, but thought I'd give it a try. When Milton came home on the weekend, he still seemed to be enchanted with the whole program. Oh, yes—They did marching and training like real soldiers, and besides, he was assigned to a sleeping room with children from three to six years old.

"Madam, do you know that some of these children are here all the time because their parents don't want them, or they don't have parents! I have to take some to the bathroom at night. I sure feel sorry for them."

"I hope they don't think I put you in there for the same reason, Milton?"

"Are you warm enough with such a chilly room?"

"No, I sleep with my coat on and sometimes a couple boys want to sleep with me because they are cold. I am going to take a couple of blankets with me mom," Milton said.

I went with him when he had to return to school. I wanted to check it once more. I was not as impressed with it as Milton seemed to be. I guess the uniform did it. I explained that my reasoning was to make sure he was safe when I was at work, as he'd be alone too many hours after school. Then I left for home.

I called Milton up one evening and was informed that he would not be able to come to the phone. He was being punished for not doing something right while they were marching.

"How are they being punished for that," I asked, as my greatest concern was his ears.

"They send them down into the coal bin and they have to shovel coal from one side to the other."

"I want to speak to the man that has charge of them—NOW!" I said angrily.

"Hello, I am their Captain," I heard on the phone a few moments later.

"Is that right? I think you are a bully—punishing children in that manner without considering first their health. I did not leave my son with you because I didn't love him or want him anymore. I was given the impression they would be given good care. I realize that there is a time to reprimand when it is in order, but not that dirty!"

"Lots of parents leave their children here and forget to come back," he said, trying to get a word in, but I was too angry.

"So, what do you do—make it rough on them?" I questioned.

"I don't happen to be that kind of parent; is that understood? Milton has a chronic ear condition, and you better see that it doesn't develop into a serious infection from all the dirt and perspiration running into his ears."

I heard him gasp at the other end of the phone.

"Yes, Madam! Goodbye," he said and hung up the phone.

When Milton came home that weekend I asked him what took place after my phone call. He was not told that I had called. The captain had come down to him before he was through shoveling the coal over to the other side and said he better come with him.

"He took me to the nurse and she cleaned my ears out and I took a bath and went to bed. The nurse has been checking my ears three times a day since then. Before that it was only when I'd come to her and ask her to look at them. Now, I know why all this attention."

Through the winter months, with so much dampness, this just caused Milton's ears to drain more and his asthma aggravated to laborious breathing. With spring just around the corner, I told my brother that I made plans to go home. He tried to discourage me, but my mind was made up. In a way it was a sad leaving for my son, but he never made a fuss when I decided what we should do.

We left by train in March when spring was coming into its own beauty. Of course Montana greeted us with its mild spring opening, too. Since I never informed anyone of my coming home, we took a taxi and surprised my brother Jim just as he was getting ready to go to work. Of course he wondered why I came home instead of waiting for school to be out first. So many questions and very few good reasons— after thinking it over I began to wonder too. Before leaving there, Mr.

West told me that my job would be waiting for me whenever I was ready to come back. I was told, by my family, that winters in Montana would not be kind to Milton either. Perhaps I should have listened to George when he said he'd get me a job in Palm Springs if I'd stay, but in my heart I thought I was doing the right thing at the time.

We were not home a week when Jim decided to move in with Eda and Jack. It was the best arrangement for all. Milton started school and I went back to work for J.C. Penny department store. When summer came, Milton worked at the swimming pool and when that closed, he got a paper route. He started school again and kept up his paper delivery, but in November Milton came down with rheumatic fever. He was in bed three months and three months of slow recovery. The cold weather was not his best friend.

"Frasinia, you ought to paint the ceiling blue like the sky and put some stars in it so the kid won't forget what the outside looks like," Mike said.

Mr. Corrall was not pleased when I took time off to take care of Milton, but he said my job would be waiting for me when I returned. Milton's education was taken care of by a tutor who came to the house three times a week. Thank God—the rheumatic fever did not leave his heart damaged. This helped me make up my mind to make a move to Arizona. I heard that it would be beneficial to his health.

In March of 1951, my lady friend Louise Metichka came to visit me from White Fish, Montana, for a few days. We had not seen each other for quite a few years, so there was a lot of reminiscing to do. Louis, Milton and I were having dinner when there was a knock on the door. Jim came in and was delighted to see Louise as they were acquainted from the past.

"Oh, by the way—the Moose Lodge is having potluck dinner tomorrow evening. Why don't you two join me there?" Jim asked.

"Should I bring something, Jim?" I asked.

"No, there will be more than enough for a few extras;" Jim was a member of the Moose Lodge.

"I'll see if I can get someone to stay with Milton, as I don't want to leave him alone yet, Jim."

"I'm sure Eda won't mind staying with him," Jim said.

She said she'd be glad to stay with Milton, providing we did not stay out too late. Well—we had no such intentions as far as we knew at the moment. I asked Jim if it would be all right to ask Fredia; she had a car.

"Sure thing, I'll see you ladies there tomorrow evening, as I have to be there in the afternoon."

He visited awhile longer and then bid us goodnight. The house didn't seem so quiet when he left, as we were all laughing and talking about the good times we had had in he past.

The next day in the evening as we walked into the Moose Lodge, Jim was on a lookout for us. He waved for us to follow him; he led us to the table set for three. He was cutting up like a host and bowed to us when taking his leave. We were laughing over such royal service when he returned with a white towel over his arm and bearing a tray with hot food. Before he left he gave me a hug and said,

"Ladies, enjoy yourselves. If you need more, just ask. Oh—if you want drinks, Steve will take care of that."

Steve was my sister's husband, working as a bartender. He was a member of the Moose Lodge, too. Then Louise spoke up,

"Frasinia, those two men keep looking at us."

"Ignore them," I said; "Oh, they may know Fredia."

Fredia said she knew one of them as he had his farm next to her place. The man smiled at her, before getting up with his friend and walking to our table. He introduced his friend to Fredia and that way we all got to meet each other. As the band was playing on the dance floor, Carl asked Fredia and Frank asked Louise. This left me sitting alone. Jim came over and we talked a while; then he said,

"Sis, I'd dance with you, but I must get back and help out with the serving."

"Oh—I don't mind, Jim; I like my food warm, besides I'd better call and see how things are at home."

They brought the girls back and left to their table. Louise and Fredia started to eat, and I went to make my phone call. It seemed everything was fine at home. Milton was in bed and Eda was crocheting. Jack left for home as he was an early to bed fellow. When I came back to the table the girls were through eating and seemed to have some kind of joke going on between them. I asked if I could be in on it.

"Sure thing, as you're the one in it."

"Really now, what have I done?" I questioned.

"Frank and Carl danced with us to ask about you."

"I hope you said something to scare them."

We were laughing. Frank and Carl walked up as a waltz was being played. Frank asked me to dance and Louise danced with Carl. While we were dancing Frank said,

"I'll be 37 years old first of April."

"You are still a young man." I said.

"I'm a construction engineer," he went on.

"That accounts for your ruddy complexion."

"Yes—I work in all kinds of weather," he said, smiling.

"I'll be 44 years old on April 20th—so you see there is quite a difference."

It seemed I was always trying to find a reason to discourage him, but his mind was made up. I told him I was going to move to Phoenix, Arizona, before next winter.

"I'll take you there." he said.

He did not waste any time but kept himself in the lamplight where I was concerned; it was a whirlwind courtship. On May 8, 1954, we were married in the church with a few friends. After the ceremony, we went to join his boss and the crew that Frank worked with and their wives for a dinner given in our honor. It was a delightful gathering and a delicious dinner. A few hours later we left on our weekend honeymoon; we both had to be back Monday morning to work.

The construction company Frank was working for had finished the job they were working on and were moving on to another site. As it was a few hundred miles from home Frank would be coming home on weekends, or whenever the weather permitted, as it was winter. I made up my mind that this was not my cup of tea, besides Gary, his youngest son, decided he wanted to live with his father. So I bought a trailer house and quit my job. We rented the house to an elderly couple. In a couple of weeks, we were ready to join Frank. He came home late Friday evening. I had things ready. He was surprised and mostly flabbergasted at my determination.

"Frasinia, I don't think the job will last that long before we'll have to move on to another one," he said.

"Well—we will just move on with you, and the children will have to adjust to different schools," I answered.

"Guess there is nothing else we can do but get ready and move this weekend," Frank said.

Saturday morning Frank hooked the trailer to the car with all adjustments that had to be done. Early Sunday morning we bid goodbye to our relatives and some early neighbors. The day was beautiful but crisp, as we pulled out from home.

The trip was trouble free as we pulled into a large trailer court in Townsend, Montana, close to the job site. It was after eight o'clock and quite dark, so all the trailer manager said was that there were accommodations for our personal needs. He also said we could get some water for drinking, and it would be better to hookup in daylight and he'd help since he knew that Frank had to be on the job by 8 a.m. So we had a candlelight dinner and then went to bed. It was good to nestle in for the night, as it had been a long and tiring day.

Frank was up just at the break of dawn. He was told the night before what lot number to put the trailer in. The boys were still in bed, but I got up with Frank. It was not very long before he had the trailer parked and was hooking up the sewer when the manager walked up.

"My, but you are an early riser, Dolack," he said.

"I wanted to have everything done before going to work." Frank said.

The electricity was plugged in and as we were cooking and heating with propane, that was taken care of too. A quick breakfast was had by all. Frank left to work and the boys were getting ready to go to school. We walked to the only school they had in Townsend. The boys were signed in and I left to look the town over and do some grocery shopping. There was a store not far from the trailer court. I bought enough food for dinner and breakfast. My thoughts were filled with what had taken place in such a short time and if I did the right thing—hoping that it would be for the best.

We met the neighbors around us and it seemed they were following jobs, too. At least the boys didn't feel alone at school. They seemed to enjoy their school. Our stay was short-lived. As I was preparing for Christmas dinner, Frank came in and said,

"We have to leave right now.

"I can serve the food right now," I said.

"No time, we must leave before the storm comes. We have to go over the Continental Divide—hopefully in daylight—so hurry!" Frank said as he left to hookup the trailer to the car.

The boys helped me to secure the things inside and we put all the dinner on the floor of the car on my side. In less than an hour we were on our way to a new challenge. Just as we pulled out the snow started to fall softly in big flakes. Since it was late in the afternoon, Frank was worried about icy roads and it certainly came to pass. In the meantime I started serving dinner. We had the turkey and all the trimmings. The boys were first to enjoy the Christmas dinner, then I. Frank had to keep his eyes on the road and hands on the steering wheel as the car was pulling a 36-foot long trailer.

Everything was going along just fine until we started over McDonald Pass, which was when the car lost its grip and stopped with the trailer blocking the road.

"Frasinia, you keep your foot on the brakes to make sure that the car won't let go and start going backwards. I am sure there is a Ranger Station close by— maybe we could get them to help us."

He walked off. It seemed in no time he was back with the Ranger, who looked at the mess and said,

"I don't think I can be of any help to you, and we are not allowed to hook on—it's against the rules."

"Well, if that's the case, I'll have to stay here all night and that is not going to help the traffic," Frank said.

With that vision in mind, the Ranger hooked his truck to the car and in a few minutes we were on our way. Frank offered to pay him, but he just wished a Merry Christmas to us all. We thanked him and wished him a most blessed holiday.

It was quite late when we drove into the trailer park. As there were accommodations, we didn't hookup the trailer, just brought in the food—Frank had his late Christmas dinner and I and the boys a second one by candle light. Next morning the sun was out bright and shiny. The snow was deep. Many people were digging out around the trailers and making paths. It seemed that most of the trailers had sewer back-ups. Frank decided that it was a poor spot to park, but as he had to go to work, we would wait until he came home. He plugged in the electricity and left for work. His first day at work was very pleasant and most of all, he met a man on the job who said he could park the trailer in his backyard. As the dinner was on the table, we ate and then started to get ready to move again.

So this is Florence, Montana, I thought. There were a few houses scattered here and there but within walking distance to Frank's work. The family, where we parked the trailer in their backyard, was pleasant and comfortable to be around. It was a lovely setting; we could hear the wind howling in the mountains and it was so quiet and peaceful below.

Spring found Frank without a job. The Construction Company was moving to Billings, Montana, to their place of business with no job available at the present time. We could have followed and waited until they had one, but we decided to move to East Helena, Montana. In a few weeks, Frank got a job with another Construction Company which lasted through the winter. The boys finished out their school year there.

We received a letter from our son-in-law, that there were quite a few job openings at Malmstrom Air Force Base and perhaps if we would come back it was possible that Frank could get one of those jobs.

Next day, we called one of the trailer movers and in a couple days we were back in Great Falls, Montana. Since our home was rented, we moved into a trailer court. Frank wasted no time to go and apply for a job. In a couple of days, he was called to come to work. A month later, I went to work at Paris department store. Milton worked at the swimming pool until it closed, and Gary worked at the Woolworth store.

Our renters moved out, so on a weekend we moved into the house. The house needed rejuvenating—indoors and out. What a challenge but a pleasing and gratifying sight when the job was finished. Winter came with a flurry; it had not been this cold for many years. Milton spent most of his time in bed with colds and earaches. I got in touch with a church in Phoenix, Arizona. They informed me of a good church going elder couple that I could depend on leaving my son with until I could join him.

Frank took one week off during the Christmas vacation. We left early one Saturday morning with the three boys. Tony, Frank's oldest son, came with us on the trip. He was making his home with his mother at the time. The trip was safe, as the highways were cleared of snow most of the time; besides God was with us. We made the trip in three days. Arriving in Phoenix late in the afternoon we started looking for a motel, one to accommodate all of us. With that out of the way—next was to find a place to eat. We found a Chinese restaurant that also served American food, so we all had a turkey dinner.

Driving around a bit, we then went back to the motel for a good night's rest. Next morning, I called the lady up; she was waiting for us to have breakfast with them. I thanked her and said we'd be over soon. When we drove into their yard, it was like coming home. I felt as though I had known them all my life. We visited a while and before we knew it, it was lunch time. They insisted we eat before we left. It was hard to leave my son behind, although he said that I'd probably be glad to leave him and be on my way. I promised to write often. Mrs. Jacobson said she would keep me informed how he did in school and his health. We said goodbye and left for the motel to pack and leave for home.

The reports about Milton's health and school work were promising. He attended the church and was quite active in it. What pleased me most of all was that he was not sick there like he was at home; this helped me make up my mind to leave him there that fall for sure. It was just what he needed as so much time was lost in bad health.

In the spring Frank went and bought a water cooler and installed it in the front window of the trailer, so we could take the heat in Arizona. Summers were always beautiful in Montana, so Milton came home after school was out in Arizona. I was happy to have him at home. He got his summer job again at the swimming pool. It was just long enough work to help him to make some pocket change before leaving for Arizona before school started. I had saved up enough money to pay to have the trailer moved to Arizona and some extra to help us over before I got a job. Frank and Gary took board and room with the people we rented the house to. Frank thought it'd be a good idea for me to check in for his line of work before he quit the job he had as jobs were hard to come by. Milton rode with the man that took the trailer and I followed two weeks later by bus, arriving there August 26, 1957.

Milton met me at the bus depot. Then we took the city bus to the place where he had parked the trailer. It wasn't very far from the people he stayed with. We had a bite to eat and then walked over to see them. It was like coming home. How nice it was to have such good friends in a strange city.

On Monday morning Milton and I went job hunting. It was cool in the morning but by the time we got to the department stores the perspiration was running down our neck and the back of my dress was plastered to my back, but this did not discourage our interviews. We went to the washrooms and made ourselves halfway presentable.

We left with a promise that they'd call us if there was an opening—different stores and same answer. Two weeks went by and no one called, but in the meantime there was a flu death in the court a couple trailers down. Milton got the flu; he was one sick boy. I called the doctor to please come and see him. He advised me to just give him aspirin and lots of liquids. His fever was up to 105 that evening. It frightened me. I stayed up all night with him and bathed him with cool water many times. By morning his fever was down and he fell asleep soundly. In a few days he was able to sit up and take nourishment. He confided in me later that he was frightened that he too would die like that man.

While Milton was recuperating, I was called to work at Goodwater's department store—afternoon shift of all things at a time like this, as I hated to leave Milton.

"Mom, I'll be just fine, just make sure to catch the right bus going down and coming back."

Well, I made it with God's help and people's kindness. Milton was awake and worrying about me. I guess we both were worrying about each other. He told me that there was a young man that came over and visited with him and asked if there was something he could do for him.

"I was not alone mom. I was outside some too."

It was a great relief to go on day shift; it helped to put our life more into perspective. Milton was feeling stronger each day. The warm climate did wonders for his ears. Right after Labor Day he started back to school, the same one he attended while living with Jacobson's.

Frank and I had been corresponding. In the meantime, I had checked for his kind of work and they informed me that he'd have to appear in person. He wrote me a letter that there was going to be a reduction in man power at Malmstrom Air Force Base and he might be one of many.

By October 19, 1957, Frank and Gary moved to Phoenix. It was nice to have the family together again. Frank was in luck; he got a job with the forest service, in line with the Government work. The pay was something else to be desired, but better than nothing.

Before Christmas, we traded our trailer as a down payment on a beautiful home in a choice location, but it was absolutely bare of the essentials like even a stove, or refrigerator—not even drapes. Well, back to the drawing board of how to stretch the budget. We had the use of the trailer for a few days until we bought a stove and refrigerator, and we picked up orange crates to sit on. Frank made a table out of boxes. We slept on the floor for awhile until we had time to shop. It was nice to have separate bedrooms to sleep in. We used paper boxes for dresser drawers on the top shelves of the clothes closet, and sat on the floor in the living room. The yard was the most complete with its fruit trees, roses and lawn. It was all worthwhile to be a little limited for comfort. Little by little we added more to our comfort and to beautify our home.

Since Frank was working for the Federal Government, he had a chance for a promotion with an increase in pay. He accepted the job which was in Flagstaff, Arizona. He came home on weekends. His next move was to Parker Dam, Arizona, in 1959 with an increase in pay, but again he was commuting on weekends.

Tony came to live with us and was attending college with Milton. Gary would be ready in the fall. All three were working after school and weekends. Milton became engaged to a lovely girl that he met at the college, and he was so in love that college became secondary, but of course with a promise that college would be attended. They were married April 30th, 1960 in a small church wedding attended by family and a few friends. The reception was at our home. Their going away honeymoon was in a honeymoon suite as a wedding gift from her father. Milton, Diane and Tony finished out that year with good intentions of going back in the fall. Milton was working steady at Goldwater's for the summer and managed a motel for free living quarters. Tony worked for Bayless grocery store and decided that he just may not go back to college.

In the fall, Frank and I drove Gary to Mexico where he would be attending college. He was to work a few hours in the proving grounds for missiles after college classes as he wanted to be a mechanical engineer. After being there a few days, and settling him down, we left for home. It was hard to leave a boy of seventeen who had never been away from home so far away for any length of time. We had so many misgivings but prayed for the best.

When we came home, it was quite late so Frank decided to sleep at home and get up early in the morning and hoped to get in, in time for work. Later I learned he made it just fine.

Tony and I were holding down the fort now. Milton and Diane were looking for a larger motel to manage. Milton was looking for a job with better pay as they were expecting a new addition in their family, so college would have to wait for awhile.

Tony got a steady job. He seemed to enjoy his work, so Frank and I thought that if later he should decide to go back to college, it was never too late. Since the children had made up their own plans, we put the house up for sale so I could join Frank. Tony informed me that he was going to rent an apartment with another young man.

We had our last Christmas dinner together in our Phoenix home. Gary was home on his vacation. It was sad in many ways to part with our lovely home. Frank had rented a three bedroom house that was available for Federal workers. The week before we were to turn our home over to the buyers, Frank came home on a weekend and we packed the self-moving van with all our belongings and he left for Parker Dam, California. I was to leave on the bus the following week.

I bid the children and our neighbors' goodbye and went to stay that night with one of my friends that I worked with at Goldwater's; she was to take me to the bus the next morning.

I arrived at Parker Dam, about three-thirty in the afternoon. Frank was to meet me after he got off work. Since I had a few hours to pass away, I checked my luggage and went to look the town over. You'd be surprised at my reaction. People were smiling and very pleasant, but they seemed amused at my lost expression. Some kind soul stopped and asked me if I was lost.

"I don't think so, but where is the main street?" I asked.

"You are standing on it," he said.

I thanked him and walked into a building that said drugstore. There was a lunch counter and a number of people sitting there. I walked up and started to order a sandwich with banana and peanut butter, and a glass of milk.

"I never heard of that kind of sandwich," he said.

"Oh, it is very good and wholesome," I said.

He went to make it for me. What I did not know was that there were wives there having lunch, wives of the men that Frank worked with, wives who thought that it was a juicy gossip to talk about in the village. I paid for the lunch and walked outside. I decided to forego looking the town over, since I was all ready on the main street. I went back to the depot and waited for Frank. It was not long before he came in and asked if I was ready to go home. Home, was it another Parker Dam? Frank must have seen the question on my face; he grinned—not saying anything, then he said.

"Let's eat before we go home."

As I had not prepared anything, knowing he hadn't had his dinner, I agreed that it was just fine with me. When we were ready to order dinner, I told him that I had had a sandwich and milk so I was not too hungry.

"Well, order a dinner anyway."

I didn't know that some of his friends were having dinner out and he wanted to make sure there would not be room for gossip. The longer I lived there I realized not to go beyond

"Good morning! How are you and your family?" if they had any, and

"Thank you! I am just fine."

They were good people but hungry for a broader life. Before entering the restaurant, Frank tried to prepare me that he had started to unpack but decided against it as he wasn't sure where I wanted to place things. The dish barrel was half empty—some on the floor and table. Thank goodness that he stopped.

The house was painted inside with antique white, which I had ordered, when they asked Frank what color I'd like. It was late in the day so we just relaxed and talked. The next morning after Frank left for work, I had lined out a chore for myself. By the time he came home, I had the cupboards lined with paper and dishes washed and put away, floors scrubbed and dinner on the table.

Frank asked if I'd like to go and meet a few of our neighbors, as he had been telling them that I was coming to join him soon. I felt rather weary and asked if we could not do it on a weekend.

"Oh, we won't be out too late."

His boss and family lived across from us, so they were the first that I met. It seemed that Frank had so much to talk about that the time went by fast. By then it was too late to go anywhere else close by. His boss's wife and I just smiled at each other.

When I got home, I declined to meet anyone else until we were settled in our new home, and that's the way it was. When the inside was finished the outside was next. Frank took care of the yard and I the flowerbeds.

On my first morning out cultivating the flowers—dry with a few roots representing flowers, Mr. Monard walked by our place on his way to work. He stopped to tell me that I was working too hard out in the hot sun.

"Mrs. Dolack, the people that lived there before you couldn't make anything grow in the ground—just isn't right."

"Well, if nothing grows, at least it will be clean, and we may just fill it up with colorful rocks," I said smiling.

He bid me good-day and walked on. I turned to my work. The sun was hot so I quit and went into the house where there was always plenty to do.

Unbeknownst to me, the women were watching me work in the yard; and wanting to meet me, they brought me flowers to plant in the yard from their places. By the time summer came around, we had the most beautiful flowers around the house and the lawn was thick like a carpet. It took a lot of watering and fertilizer.

Gary came back from school for the summer, besides he decided that it was not for him. Back to the drawing board, he got himself a job at Metropolitan Water Company for the summer. By the time fall semester came he was ready to attend a college in Blythe, California. It was not only a two year college, he did very well. He had enough credits to enroll in Humboldt State College in Arcadia, California. While going to college there, he got a job at Saint Joseph Hospital and that is where he decided to become a Hospital Administrator. He got his Bachelor's degree at Humboldt State College and Master's degree in Washington, D.C.

Tony became Assistant Manager in the Bayless grocery store. He married a lovely girl and they had two children—a boy and a girl. They lived in Phoenix, Arizona. Milton became a computer analyst and supervisor for the Public Services in Phoenix, Arizona. All three of our boys were successful and had their own homes, lovely wives, and children.

Our move to Arizona proved to be beneficial to all—health wise and jobs. Our daughter Marlene and her husband John had three children and lived in Gresham, Oregon. They did well. Their children brought pride and joy to all of us—honor students in school and good American citizens.

The six years we lived at Parker Dam were pleasant and some

made their own problems, as the saying goes—"What we sow is what we reap." We had many enjoyable potluck dinners at the community hall. Each woman was asked to bring a certain dish, which together, was a beautiful delicious banquet. Of course each tried to outdo the other using favorite recipes.

We had a contest on the most interesting handmade hat. I wrapped clear plastic wrap in a most fashionable way around my head and pinned two roses on one side. When I came in all eyes were on me except the two heads that were whispering together, which I overhead. They were such buddy friends.

Mrs. Cook was one of the women that most of the women looked up to in the village. Her hat was not all homemade, just decorated with paper flowers. Don't worry, if she were planning to say anything, I'd fix her. I smiled at them as I walked past.

I really only had a couple of lady friends. As I walked to their table and sat down, I felt like an outsider and out of place. Carol and Evelyn both spoke up at the same time,

"You should win. There isn't another hat like yours in here."

"Not if they can help it." Of course they knew who I meant.

"It will go by applause," Carol said.

Each one of us that had a hat got up to model our creations. The applause was loud and noisy when I modeled my hat. Mrs. Goodie and I were tied, so we had to model again. Same reason—the decision came to a tie. Our pictures were taken, but somehow I never was on the same picture, and of course, they just didn't turn out.

Oh, there was another club formed by a group called "Throw the Key into the Ring." We just never joined that Russian roulette, as nature has a way of backfiring. Not that we were never asked. They approached my husband and he related it to me.

"I told them I didn't think you'd go for it."

"And you are right! Let's drop the subject and have dinner with a clean mind," I said.

So much for our social life—we found more enjoyment visiting our children and having them visit us, besides taking a trip to other places of interest. We looked forward to seeing our brothers, sisters, and friends.

Frank bought a boat—an outboard motor boat. It was a pleasure for a while. Tony, Gary and Frank learned to water ski. It was beautiful to go out on the Colorado River for such pleasures. There were many others—enjoying the sport too—until it became infected with big city folks, who wanted to get away from it all on weekends and let their hair down. There was just no room for the local people on the river on weekends. The resorts were filled and besides the river banks were lined with cars if they could possibly drive into the area and sleep on the ground.

The Metropolitan Water Company doctor was one busy weekend doctor. He treated snake bites, rock cuts, and bruises from fighting and wild boat dodging that threw people into the water with churning propellers ready to slice. Yes, some poor soul lost his head. It took that, to put restrictions on wild gang play!

Thank God they did not invade our swimming area and picnic grounds. Frank sold the boat shortly after Gary left for Washington, D.C. to go to college. He felt that it would be safer for all concerned.

In 1966, Frank was transferred to Needles, California. It seemed as if we just made friends with some interesting people at work and in church when it was time to move again. His next move was to Parker, Arizona, in 1969. We no sooner got settled when an order came three months later that we had to move to Yuma, Arizona. The contract fell through, because the Indians agreed to disagree on the contract which would have been for seven years.

Before we moved, John, Marlene and their three children were on their vacation, so we had the pleasure of their company for a week. While the vacationers were with us, Milton, Diane and their two children came on the weekend to visit also, besides we had not seen each other for years.

When they left on their last leg of vacation to Los Angeles and

Disneyland, we made plans to go to Yuma the next day and look for a place to live. A couple of days were allowed to employees to look for living quarters. We were fortunate to find a place on the first day we were there. The place needed painting badly. Frank said he'd see that they would do it before the movers came. Next we got in touch with the movers, who said they'd be there as soon as we gave them a call. We picked up a bunch of discarded boxes at their company, for I had disposed of all, thinking we were settled for a long time. The Government paid for the moving and if we did our own packing, we got paid for that. I always did the packing and Frank helped. It was nice to get a tidy sum—enough for a good vacation.

Well, here we were in Yuma, Arizona—settled down, but on the lookout for a good buy.

HOUSE HUNTING

We arrived February 14, 1970—in Yuma, Arizona. After months of looking for a house, we awakened one lovely Sunday morning and saw an advertisement in the listings of "Homes for Sale." We called the woman realtor with the listing; she said she'd meet us there in an hour. While waiting for her, my husband Frank stooped over to pick a week in the front yard.

"Honey, you behave like an owner," I said laughing.

"I just think people should keep their yard clean," he said with a sheepish grin.

We both laughed as the realtor drove up. After greeting each other, she unlocked the front door and it turned out to be the entrance to an enclosed backyard. What a lovely secluded place. The patio had a bamboo roof covering and a fish pond with goldfish swimming at the end of it.

I do believe that the sound of the waterfall sold the place for us. The house wasn't any larger than the one we had lived in except it had an extra bathroom. The house was being sold with all the furniture. We had a houseful of our own furniture, but that did not stop us from buying the place. We stored all the furniture in one of the largest bedrooms until we were ready to sell it. The rest of the place was scoured from corner to corner and ceiling down before we brought in our furniture.

Frank enlarged the utility shed and carport for two cars, which involved more concrete pouring and extending the carport roof. His next project was removing the old bamboo from the existing roof and replacing it with new. It really looked nice. Now, he started on the outside of the house, scraping loose stucco, patching and painting.

The copper color with white trim was a good setting for the desert scenery. The front door was painted flaming coral with black Chinese scrolls—which made the entrance most attractive. By now the heat of the desert was upon us.

I had to force myself to start on real house cleaning; it seemed impossible to visualize that it had been anything but brown stained wall with foul tobacco smoke stains. Cleaning had to be done before painting could even begin. It was a blessing that Frank's sister Mary and her husband Peter Hilt were visiting us just then from Montana. It was their second winter in Arizona. They were a retired couple. So Peter and Mary not only helped us move in, but they got in on the cleaning part too. Mary helped with cooking and washing up things close to the floor. As for me, I reached as high as I could. It was so saturated with tobacco smoke that I would get sick to my stomach. By the time I got through washing inside the cupboards, clothes closets and walls and generally the whole of the inside, I'd had it. Besides getting sick, I had a very sore back for almost six weeks.

Peter and Mary stayed with us for two weeks. Such dolls they were! Peter had emphysema and couldn't really do strenuous work, but he went out of his way to do whatever was possible for him to do. They had a self-contained home on a truck; this was their home away from home. In March they would leave for Montana, stopping here and there just so they'd get back in time to do their income taxes, besides spring started to spring there about that time. Montana springs and summers are most beautiful.

Finally, the escrow papers were completed, and we became legal owners. Now, we could put the excess furniture up for sale, and besides my strength returned and I didn't feel like I was dragging myself out of bed each morning. The days began to ring again—nice sound.

It was amazing how simple it was selling the furniture. God must have been with us and the people had need of secondhand furniture. It seemed the advertisement hardly got in the paper when people started coming by. In a few days the furniture was gone.

Frank had been planning to start outside painting before the Arizona heat set in, so we rushed to get ahead of it. He took all the old bamboo down from the patio and repaired all the wood then we painted it. After the paint dried we replaced with new bamboo. The house exterior was next. We scraped, sanded, patched, and puttied, and sanded again. Two coats of paint were required and a third on the sunny side. It did look nice, but we were two very tired people and we treated ourselves by going out to dinner.

The interior of the house was next. Each day Frank came home from work, I'd have more work ready. He was the official painter. Can you just visualize painting with oversized furniture in a small house? I'd cover the furniture pieces, and the floor, but heaven help us with his speed—I'd try my best to keep him from dragging the covering down with his feet. He swore that I placed obstacles in his way just to make his job harder. I couldn't believe my ears, or eyes—it was like a nightmare. If anyone looked in through the windows, it must have been quite a show for them. Aye!—woman and man racing with the time. The only time he'd pause was for a drink of water—I'd give him—encouraging him to drink it slowly and relax a bit; in my own defense, I assure you, so I could cover the furniture. Oh, my! His drinking was faster then my covering. I prayed that the instruction on the paint can was right, that one coat would do the job. No such luck—it took two and three coats in most places. I told Frank I'd do the cupboards and the woodwork while he was at work.

Finally the job was finished; we were proud of it and only tried to remember the pleasant part of it all—like the days when Frank would say we had both had it and let's go out and have dinner. It was so nice to relax, even if we felt our aches and pains from the workout. There just wasn't any exercise to compete with that, at least not the way the Dolack's did it.

The front yard was a scene of desert with cactus arrangement and male date tree. Inside of the enclosed area was a beautiful assortment of desert cactus arranged in borders against the wall of the utility shed and along the dividing fence of our neighbors' and the alley fence. Alongside the patio where the fish pond was were lovely shrubbery and climbing ferns. With three small areas of green grass, sprinklers made watering simpler for the lovely big bottle tree, orange tree and big shade tree. Our neighbors' trees across the alley and on both sides of us made our place look like we lived in the woods. The big window overlooking the patio gave the appearance of another room. Sounds like I just might like it—I did! I did!

The sound of the waterfall in the fish pond gave one the feeling of a babbling mountain stream—so relaxing and soothing—very good for one's soul. I spent many hours doing my art lessons there. One evening when Frank came home from work, he said a rumor was going around that some of the families would be moved to a new location. As it happened, we were one of them. Since we did not know how long we'd be gone, we decided to sell our place. I hoped whoever got it would enjoy it as much as we did.

Our new location was in Blythe, California. Frank had to go there the following week to start his new job, which was the same except different location. I stayed behind to sell the house. Now, all we had to do was wait until it sold—then great joy packing—not my cup of tea, but it is one way of finding out what's lost and getting rid of the accumulation—which happens in the best of families. Accumulation, we certainly had. I decided to advertise a sale for the following weekend. Frank would be home to enjoy being salesman. He did very well. What he did not sell was given to the church. We were told later that the church did well, too.

The following week, I started to pack, keeping the boxes confined to one room. We had many interested people in our house, but the right buyer did not appear yet, as mother would say.

One weekend, Frank came home and said he had a chance to rent a two bedroom apartment and wondered if I'd mind living in it. There were washing facilities and a swimming pool. And he said we could drive down that weekend to see it. Well, I was ready for an outing, besides the realtor had the key to show our house to potential buyers. We called her up and it was fine with her. After having breakfast, we left, planning to be back that evening.

It was a lovely trip and the apartment was fine. We rented the place and went out to have dinner.

"Tomorrow when I leave for work, I'll take bed and bedding and a few facilities to get by until you come. I'll move out of the motel and into the apartment," Frank said.

When he returned home the following weekend, the place was sold—just waiting for a few signatures. The movers were coming in the morning to load up our belongings and leave for Blythe Sunday morning. We turned the place over late Saturday evening to the new owners. We got ourselves a motel for the night, cleaned up and went to have dinner.

The next morning we left for Blythe to be there before the movers got there. Yeah! We beat them by one hour. As we were waiting for the movers, we got a call. Peter Hilt's dad had passed away. What a sad message—a fine person—that he was. He would not be forgotten.

If our foresight was as good as our hindsight, we would have kept the house and just rented it. We lived in Blythe one year and were told we'd have to move back to Yuma.

We took the time allowed to drive to Yuma to find a place to rent. In luck again, we rented a lovely three bedroom home. As I had been packing the past couple weeks, we were waiting for the movers who said they would be over in a couple days. Many of the men were retired and others transferred. Frank put in for disability retirement, but he didn't think he'd get it—even though he'd had many painful days, months, and years at work. He had neck injuries, he'd acquired years back on the job, which finally got worse. The doctors said that about 85% of the vertebras in his neck were deteriorating.

We were in Yuma about three months when he came home from

work one day and said,

"I got retirement papers. I don't have to go to work anymore. July 1973—well, what's next—should we just stay here or move?"

In 1963, we had purchased a place in northern California, close to McKinleyville, with great intentions of making our home there when Frank retired. We'd had the place rented all these years. It had a two room building on the property, and being a college town, we had no trouble renting it.

We decided to move and build onto our exiting building and retire there. I was getting to be quite an expert on packing, but this time I was not getting paid for it. We called my brother George and asked if we could store our furniture at his place of business until our place was finished. He said, "Yes," he had an extra empty room. We took just enough with us to manage until our place was enlarged.

We arrived August 28, 1973—rented an apartment, as our place was rented. We gave our renter 30 days to move out. In the meantime, Frank and I came over every day to clean up the yard. There was years of garbage grown over by the earth and grass. It looked like they used the yard for a garbage disposal—whichever way their throwing went. I was so furious to think that we had to clean such a mess when it wasn't of our doing. The renter must have sensed my disapproval as she made herself scarce when we were around.

I received a letter from my sister Mary asking if she could come and stay with us. She had been trying to find a place to settle in that had more mild weather than Montana. Of course, we said yes. So we found a house for rent and moved in. It was fun for all of us, as Mary liked to cook, which left me with more time to help Frank.

The irony of it all is that it rained almost from the last day of August to February 12, 1974. The sun would come out momentarily. One thing, the rain was warm. Building was out of the question for the present time. The rain was turning off Frank's desire to make our retirement home there. He felt better in a drier climate. Mary decided it was not for her either. She made plans to leave before New Years to go to her daughter Stella's place in Burbank, California, for a visit.

We had cleaned and painted the place inside, put a rug on the kitchen floor and connected an apartment size electric cooking range. Frank put in the septic tank to make things more modern. In the utility room, he installed a hot water heater, commode, wash bowel, and a shower. Our water was piped in by electricity from the spring into a large water tank.

Since Mary was leaving, we decided to move into our own little place. We just couldn't see paying such high rent. We moved out of the house January 1, 1974. It was a cozy place and clean, best of all no rent and very little electricity to pay. Hardly a day went by that someone wouldn't stop in and ask if it was for rent. Depressed following days of constant rain, Frank announced,

"I can't stand this rain; let's move to Los Angeles."

We rented the place to a young couple on the morning of February 14, 1974 and left with a loaded U-haul to Van Nuys, California, to move into my brother's house that he had on his business property, right where our furniture was stored. It was nice being close to people one loves.

By 1976 the smog, car noise, and planes got to us—something that we couldn't do anything about was holding us there, and after all, we were retired people. The only thing I missed leaving was brother George, sister Raya, and the rest of my nieces and nephews. We enjoyed getting together.

So back again we went to northern California. This time it was a beautiful time of the year and we had our plans drawn out for the addition to the house. We came with the bare necessities again—June 28, 1976. By July 30, 1976 the two extra rooms were built on and painted inside. While the carpet was being laid, Frank took the bus to Van Nuys to bring the furniture.

My brother Maurice and his family came to help us move the furniture in when Frank drove into the yard. Before many hours passed, it was all done and in place. This called for a nice dinner, so we all got ready and went out.

The air was refreshingly cool and sweet with the view of the Pacific Ocean and its ever changing scenery. Yes, we did have cooler weather there. The fog and rain seemed to be reduced to a more moderate state.

We were blessed that our children were all married with eight grandchildren who gave us much joy and pride. All are honorable young people and good American citizens. When I looked up into the sky, I felt like the cloud that is forever moving....

W h a t I s N e x t G O D!

MOLDING THE YOUTH

Yes, youth are what we make them. We corrupt them with our glances and smiles by putting into it that which only motivates lust and once the lust is loose there is no telling what length it goes before it is stopped. It is like a chain reaction of quick—lightning across the sky.

Instead of suppressing such unhealthy motives when we see them in the children, adults or if someone makes such advances to our families their self—I am sure we'd make better friends and a safer life for others and ourselves besides not mentioning the fact of less broken homes, if we only took time to think and correct the wrong before it got out of hand.

Have you ever stopped to think that someone may be doing just this very thing to your daughter, son, wife or husband? How would you really feel if this was taking place? Or doesn't it matter to you?" Or are you one?" Only you may have another name for it— let's see, oh, sex appeal!

Well, I think that if you are gifted with an inner radiation and joy of life, God meant us to use it wisely and to bring out the good in people so they would walk tall instead of crawl.

1—Often under our nose 2—Adults with experienced eye
3—Seducing a youth with his look
4—Adults plant the first seed—an excuse for their purpose on this earth
5—Second seed is a seed of distortion to true reason of life
6—Adults holding on to youth
7—Corrupting them with their thoughtless ways

8—Instead of cultivating them like a beautiful flower, they spray with doubt and corrupt the body and mind

9—There would be less crime if adults would see further than their own nose

10—We must take inventory of our souls and find where the fault lies

11—We must bear in mind that every youth is someone's loving child

12—Stay on earth is short so why not start cultivating instead of undermining

"COULD BE YOURS"

A question is asked and an answer is uttered that is so depressing to one's soul. When, I master a goal, it loses its importance and I have no need of it any more. How can I explain, that it is just me—new goals and ventures, I must attain? You mean, regardless of how it may affect other people? The answer—a shrug of the shoulders.

Projecting the reason for our existence—indestructible

OCTOBER 16, 2006

I was born April 20, 1910 in the resort community of Crimea, near the Black Sea in Russia. My parents were Duna or Dena (Yavdekia Mousyevna) and Gregory (Hrehori Sandovich Letsoef) Letz. (Last name Letz was assigned at Ellis Island when the family immigrated to the United States.)

Time has flown by, and I must try to continue my memories. Beginning of the year 2000, Frank, not feeling well, felt we must move to a warm climate. We sold our home in northern California and bought Maurice's home at a retirement village in Henderson, Nevada. (My grandson Mike remodeled our new home and made it most pleasant.)

After only one year, we had a terrible car accident, placing us in the hospital. Grandson Mike and Cathy wanted us closer, enabling them to help us easier. We sold our home in Henderson and moved into an assisted living apartment in Las Vegas (2002).

Frank found that our move south didn't seem to help his health at all. By 2004, Frank had several stays in a hospital and ended up in a nursing home.

In June, 2004—we flew to Oregon. Frank stayed in the same nursing home as Marlene's husband did before he passed away. I am living with my daughter Marlene.

Frank passed away June 23, 2004—a week after moving to

Oregon. His burial was in Montana's Veterans Cemetery in July.

Here I am with all my brothers and sisters gone from the original family. I do have four children and their spouses, eleven grandchildren, twenty-one great-grandchildren and numerous nephews and nieces to love.

GOD HAS BEEN GOOD!